LOC

C000072503

FIFTY-SEVENTH EDITION
2015

The complete guide to all
Locomotives which operate on
the national railway network
and Eurotunnel

Robert Pritchard & Peter Hall

ISBN 978 1909 431 12 6

© 2014. Platform 5 Publishing Ltd, 52 Broadfield Road, Sheffield, S8 0XJ,
England.

Printed in England by Berforts Information Press, Eynsham, Oxford.

CONTENTS

PROVISION OF INFORMATION

This book has been compiled with care to be as accurate as possible, but in some cases information is not easily available and the publisher cannot be held responsible for any errors or omissions. We would like to thank the companies and individuals which have been co-operative in supplying information to us. The authors of this series of books are always pleased to receive notification from readers of any inaccuracies readers may find in the series, to enhance future editions. Please send comments to:

Robert Pritchard, Platform 5 Publishing Ltd, 52 Broadfield Road, Sheffield, S8 0XJ, England.

e-mail: robert@platform5.com   **Tel:** 0114 255 2625   **Fax:** 0114 255 2471.
This book is updated to information received by 6 October 2014.

UPDATES

This book is updated to the Stock Changes given in **Today's Railways UK 155** (November 2014). Readers are therefore advised to update this book from the official Platform 5 Stock Changes published every month in **Today's Railways UK** magazine, starting with issue 156.

The Platform 5 magazine Today's Railways UK contains news and rolling stock information on the railways of Great Britain and Ireland and is published on the second Monday of every month. For further details of Today's Railways UK, please see the advertisement on the back cover of this book.

Front cover photograph: New DRS 68004 "Rapid" passes Hemel Hempstead hauling Greater Anglia Mark 3 12118 from Wolverton Works to Norwich on 20/08/14.   **Alisdair Anderson**

BRITAIN'S RAILWAY SYSTEM

INFRASTRUCTURE & OPERATION

Britain's national railway infrastructure is owned by a "not for dividend" company, Network Rail. In September 2014 Network Rail was classified a public sector company, being described by the Government as a "public sector arm's-length body of the Department for Transport".

Many stations and maintenance depots are leased to and operated by Train Operating Companies (TOCs), but some larger stations remain under Network Rail control. The only exception is the infrastructure on the Isle of Wight: Island Line was the only franchise that included the maintenance of the infrastructure as well as the operation of passenger services. As Island Line is now part of the South West Trains franchise, both the infrastructure and trains are operated by South West Trains.

Trains are operated by TOCs over Network Rail, regulated by access agreements between the parties involved. In general, TOCs are responsible for the provision and maintenance of the locomotives, rolling stock and staff necessary for the direct operation of services, whilst Network Rail is responsible for the provision and maintenance of the infrastructure and also for staff to regulate the operation of services.

The Department for Transport is the franchising authority for the national network, with Transport Scotland overseeing the award of the ScotRail franchise. Railway Franchise holders (TOCs) can take commercial risks, although some franchises are known as "management contracts", where ticket revenues pass directly to the DfT. Concessions (such as London Overground) see the operator paid a fee to run the service, usually within tightly specified guidelines. Operators running a Concession would not normally take commercial risks, although there are usually penalties and rewards in the contract.

During 2012 the letting of new franchises was suspended pending a review of the franchise system. The process was restarted in 2013 but it is going to take a number of years to catch-up and several franchises are receiving short-term extensions (or "Direct Awards") in the meantime.

DOMESTIC PASSENGER TRAIN OPERATORS

The large majority of passenger trains are operated by the TOCs on fixed-term franchises. Franchise expiry dates are shown in the list of franchisees below:

Franchise	*Franchisee*	*Trading Name*
Chiltern	Deutsche Bahn (Arriva) (until 31 December 2021)	**Chiltern Railways**

Chiltern Railways operates a frequent service between London Marylebone, Banbury and Birmingham Snow Hill, with some peak trains extending to Kidderminster. There are also regular services from Marylebone to Stratford-upon-Avon and to Aylesbury Vale Parkway via Amersham (along the London Underground Metropolitan Line). The fleet consists of DMUs of Classes 121 (used on the Princes Risborough–Aylesbury route), 165, 168 and 172 plus a number of loco-hauled rakes used on some of the Birmingham route trains, worked by Class 67s hired from DB Schenker.

Cross-Country

Deutsche Bahn (Arriva)
(until 31 March 2016)*

CrossCountry

Franchise extension to be negotiated to November 2019.

CrossCountry operates a network of long distance services between Scotland, North-East England and Manchester to the South-West of England, Reading, Southampton, Bournemouth and Guildford, centred on Birmingham New Street. These trains are mainly formed of diesel Class 220/221 Voyagers, supplemented by a small number of HSTs on the NE–SW route. Inter-urban services also link Nottingham, Leicester and Stansted Airport with Birmingham and Cardiff. These use Class 170 DMUs.

East Midlands

Stagecoach Group plc
(until 31 March 2015)*

East Midlands Trains

Franchise extension to be negotiated to October 2017.

EMT operates a mix of long distance high speed services on the Midland Main Line (MML), from London St Pancras to Sheffield (Leeds at peak times and some extensions to York/Scarborough) and Nottingham, and local and regional services ranging from the Norwich–Liverpool route to Nottingham–Skegness, Nottingham–Mansfield–Worksop, Nottingham–Matlock and Derby–Crewe. It also operates local services in Lincolnshire. Trains on the MML are worked by a fleet of Class 222 DMUs and ten HSTs, whilst the local and regional fleet consists of DMU Classes 153, 156 and 158.

Essex Thameside

National Express Group plc
(until 8 November 2029)

c2c

c2c operates an intensive, principally commuter, service from London Fenchurch Street to Southend and Shoeburyness via both Upminster and Tilbury. The fleet consists entirely of Class 357 EMUs. In 2014 c2c won a new 15-year franchise that promised to introduce 17 new 4-car EMUs from 2019.

Greater Western

First Group plc
(until 20 September 2015)

First Great Western

Franchise extension currently being negotiated.

First Great Western operates long distance trains from London Paddington to South Wales, the West Country and Worcester and Hereford. In addition there are frequent trains along the Thames Valley corridor to Newbury and Oxford, plus local and regional trains throughout the South-West including the Cornish, Devon and Thames Valley branches, the Reading–Gatwick North Downs line and Cardiff–Portsmouth Harbour and Bristol–Weymouth regional routes. A fleet of 53 HSTs is used on the long-distance trains, with DMUs of Classes 165 and 166 used on the North Downs and Thames Valley routes and Class 180s used alongside HSTs on the Cotswold Line to Worcester and Hereford. Classes 143, 150, 153 and 158 are used on local and regional trains in the South-West. A small fleet of four Class 57s is maintained to work the overnight "Cornish Riviera" Sleeper service between London and Penzance.

Greater Anglia

Abellio (NS)
(until 19 October 2016)

Abellio Greater Anglia

Abellio Greater Anglia operates main line trains between London Liverpool Street, Ipswich and Norwich and local trains across Norfolk, Suffolk and parts of Cambridgeshire. It also runs local and commuter services into Liverpool Street from the Great Eastern (including Southend, Braintree and Clacton) and West Anglia (including Cambridge and Stansted Airport) routes. It operates a varied fleet of Class 90s with loco-hauled Mark 3 sets, DMUs of Classes 153, 156 and 170 and EMUs of Classes 315, 317, 321, 360 and 379. London Overground is due to take over some suburban services from Liverpool Street (to Chingford, Cheshunt and Enfield) in May 2015.

| **Integrated Kent** | Govia Ltd (Go-Ahead/Keolis)
(until 24 June 2018) | **Southeastern** |

Southeastern operates all services in the South-East London suburbs, the whole of Kent and part of Sussex, which are primarily commuter services to London. It also operates domestic high speed trains on HS1 from St Pancras to Ashford, Ramsgate, Dover and Faversham with additional peak services on other routes. EMUs of Classes 375, 376, 465 and 466 are used, along with Class 395s on the High Speed trains.

| **InterCity East Coast** | Directly Operated Railways
(until 31 March 2015) | **East Coast** |

Currently run on an interim basis by DfT management company Directly Operated Railways (trading as East Coast). This arrangement is due to continue until a new franchise is let to the private sector, with the new franchise currently planned to start on 1 April 2015.

East Coast operates frequent long distance trains on the East Coast Main Line between London King's Cross, Leeds, York, Newcastle and Edinburgh, with less frequent services to Bradford, Harrogate, Skipton, Hull, Lincoln, Glasgow, Aberdeen and Inverness. A mixed fleet of Class 91s and 30 Mark 4 sets, and 14 HST sets, are used on these trains.

| **InterCity West Coast** | Virgin Rail Group Ltd
(until 31 March 2017) | **Virgin Trains** |

Virgin operates long distance services along the West Coast Main Line from London Euston to Birmingham/Wolverhampton, Manchester, Liverpool and Glasgow using Class 390 Pendolino EMUs. It also operates Class 221 Voyagers on the Euston–Chester–Holyhead route, whilst a mixture of 221s and 390s are used on the Euston–Birmingham–Glasgow/Edinburgh route. One rake of Mark 3 loco-hauled stock is also leased, and normally used on Thursdays and Fridays (this was due to be returned to Porterbrook at the end of October 2014).

| **London Rail** | MTR/Deutsche Bahn
(until 12 November 2016) | **London Overground** |

This is a Concession and is different from other rail franchises, as fares and service levels are set by Transport for London instead of by the DfT.

London Overground operates services on the Richmond–Stratford North London Line and the Willesden Junction–Clapham Junction West London Line, plus the new East London Line from Highbury & Islington to New Cross and New Cross Gate, with extensions to Clapham Jn (via Denmark Hill), Crystal Palace and West Croydon. It also runs services from London Euston to Watford Junction. All these use Class 378 EMUs whilst Class 172 DMUs are used on the Gospel Oak–Barking route.

| **Merseyrail Electrics** | Serco/Abellio (NS)
(until 19 July 2028) | **Merseyrail** |

Under the control of Merseytravel PTE instead of the DfT. Franchise reviewed every five years to fit in with the Merseyside Local Transport Plan.

Merseyrail operates services between Liverpool and Southport, Ormskirk, Kirkby, Hunts Cross, New Brighton, West Kirby, Chester and Ellesmere Port, all worked by EMUs of Classes 507 and 508.

Northern Rail

Serco/Abellio (NS)
(until 1 February 2016)

Northern

Northern operates a range of inter-urban, commuter and rural services throughout the North of England, including those around the cities of Leeds, Manchester, Sheffield, Liverpool and Newcastle. The network extends from Chathill in the north to Nottingham in the south, and Cleethorpes in the east to St Bees in the west. Long distance services include Leeds–Carlisle, Middlesbrough–Carlisle and York–Blackpool North. The operator uses a large fleet of DMUs of Classes 142, 144, 150, 153, 155, 156 and 158 plus EMU Classes 321, 322, 323 and 333.

ScotRail

First Group plc
(until 31 March 2015)

ScotRail

Abellio has won the contract to operate the ScotRail franchise from April 2015.

ScotRail provides almost all passenger services within Scotland and also trains from Glasgow to Carlisle via Dumfries, some of which extend to Newcastle (jointly operated with Northern). The company also operates the overnight Caledonian Sleeper services between London and Glasgow, Edinburgh, Inverness, Aberdeen and Fort William. In addition to the Sleeper loco-hauled stock (hauled by Class 67s and 90s hired from DB Schenker), the company operates a large fleet of DMUs of Classes 156, 158 and 170 and EMU Classes 314, 318, 320, 334 and 380. One loco-hauled rake is also used on a Fife Circle commuter train, hauled by a Class 67.

South Central

Govia Ltd (Go-Ahead/Keolis)
(until 25 July 2015)

Southern

Upon termination of the Southern franchise in July 2015 it is to be combined with the new Thameslink, Southern & Great Northern franchise (also operated by Govia).

Southern operates predominantly commuter services between London, Surrey and Sussex, as well as services along the South Coast between Southampton, Brighton, Hastings and Ashford, and also the cross-London service linking South Croydon and Milton Keynes. It also operates metro services in South London and Gatwick Express, which is a premium non-stop service between London Victoria and Gatwick Airport. Class 171 DMUs are used on Brighton–Ashford and London Bridge–Uckfield services, whilst all other services are in the hands of EMUs of Classes 313, 377, 442 and 455.

South Western

Stagecoach Group plc
(until 3 February 2017)*

South West Trains

Franchise extension to be negotiated to April 2019.

South West Trains operates trains from London Waterloo to destinations across the South and South-West including Woking, Basingstoke, Southampton, Portsmouth, Salisbury, Exeter, Reading and Weymouth as well as suburban services from Waterloo. SWT also runs services between Ryde and Shanklin on the Isle of Wight, using former London Underground 1938 stock (Class 483). The rest of the fleet consists of DMU Classes 158 and 159 and EMU Classes 444, 450, 455, 456 and 458.

Thameslink & Great Northern

Govia Ltd (Go-Ahead/Keolis)
(until 19 September 2021)

Govia Thameslink Railway

The Southern franchise will be combined with Govia Thameslink Railway from July 2015.

Govia operates this franchise as a management contract. GTR operates trains on the Thameslink route between Bedford and Brighton via central London and also on the Sutton and Wimbledon loops. A joint service with Southeastern is also operated to Sevenoaks, Orpington and Ashford. GTR also runs services on the Great Northern route from London King's Cross and Moorgate to Welwyn Garden City, Hertford North, Peterborough, Cambridge and Kings Lynn. The fleet consists of EMU Classes 319 and 377 (and 387 from 2015) for the Thameslink route services and Classes 313, 317, 321 and 365 for the Great Northern route services.

Trans-Pennine Express	First Group/Keolis (until 1 April 2015)	**TransPennine Express**

Franchise extension to be negotiated to February 2016.

TransPennine Express operates predominantly long distance inter-urban services linking major cities across the North of England, along with Edinburgh and Glasgow in Scotland. The main services are Manchester Airport/Manchester Piccadilly–Newcastle/Middlesbrough/Hull plus Liverpool–Scarborough and Liverpool–Newcastle along the North Trans-Pennine route via Huddersfield, Leeds and York, and Manchester Airport–Cleethorpes along the South Trans-Pennine route via Sheffield. TPE also operates Manchester Airport–Blackpool/Barrow/Windermere/Edinburgh/Glasgow. The fleet consists of DMU Classes 170 (used on the Hull and Cleethorpes routes) and 185 and also new Class 350 EMUs used on Manchester Airport–Scotland services.

Wales & Borders	Deutsche Bahn (Arriva) (until 14 October 2018)*	**Arriva Trains Wales**

The franchise agreement includes the provision for the term to be further extended by mutual agreement by up to five years beyond October 2018. Management of the franchise is devolved to the Welsh Government, but DfT is still the procuring authority.

Arriva Trains Wales operates a mix of long distance, regional and local services throughout Wales, including the Valley Lines network of lines around Cardiff, and also through services to the English border counties and to Manchester and Birmingham. The fleet consists of DMUs of Classes 142, 143, 150, 158 and 175 and one loco-hauled rake used on a premium Welsh Government sponsored service on the Cardiff–Holyhead route, hauled by a Class 67.

West Midlands	Govia Ltd (Go-Ahead/Keolis) (until 19 September 2015)*	**London Midland**

Franchise extension to be negotiated to June 2017.

London Midland operates long distance and regional services from London Euston to Northampton and Birmingham/Crewe and also between Birmingham and Liverpool as well as local and regional services around Birmingham, including to Stratford-upon-Avon, Worcester, Hereford, Redditch and Shrewsbury. It also operates the Bedford–Bletchley and Watford Jn–St Albans Abbey branches. The fleet consists of DMU Classes 150, 153, 170 and 172 and EMU Classes 321, 323 and 350.

* Franchise agreement includes provision for an extension of up to seven 4-week reporting periods.

The following operators run non-franchised services (* special summer services only):

Operator	Trading Name	Route
BAA	Heathrow Express	London Paddington–Heathrow Airport
First Hull Trains	First Hull Trains	London King's Cross–Hull
Grand Central	Grand Central	London King's Cross–Sunderland/ Bradford Interchange
North Yorkshire Moors Railway Enterprises	North Yorkshire Moors Railway	Pickering–Grosmont–Whitby/ Battersby
West Coast Railway Company	West Coast Railway Company	Birmingham–Stratford-upon-Avon* Fort William–Mallaig* York–Wakefield–York–Scarborough*

INTERNATIONAL PASSENGER OPERATIONS

Eurostar operates passenger services between the UK and mainland Europe.

Eurostar International, established in 2010, is jointly owned by the SNCF (the national operator of France), 55%, SNCB (the national operator of Belgium), 5% and HM Treasury, 40%. The 40% UK stake was transferred from London & Continental Railways (LCR) to HM Treasury in 2014. LCR had bought British Rail's interest in Eurostar at the time of the UK railway privatisation in 1996.

In addition, a service for the conveyance of accompanied road vehicles through the Channel Tunnel is provided by the tunnel operating company, Eurotunnel.

FREIGHT TRAIN OPERATIONS

The following operators operate freight services or empty passenger stock workings under "Open Access" arrangements:

Colas Rail: In addition to its On-Track Machines and infrastructure activities, Colas Rail operates a number of freight flows, including steel, coal and timber. Colas Rail has a small but varied fleet consisting of Class 37s, 47s, 56s, 60s, 66s and 70s. The ten Class 60s were acquired from DBS in 2014 and initially five are being returned to service.

DB Schenker Rail (UK): Still the biggest freight operator in the country, DBS (formerly EWS before being bought by DB) has seen some of its core traffic lost to competitors in recent years. It still provides a large number of infrastructure trains to Network Rail and operates coal, steel, intermodal and aggregate trains nationwide. The core fleet is Class 66s. Of the original 250 ordered 176 are still used in the UK, with the remainder having moved to DB's French and Polish operations, although some of the French locos do return to the UK when major maintenance is required. A fleet of around 25 Class 60s are also used on heavier trains.

DBS's six Class 59/2s are used alongside the Mendip Rail 59/0s and 59/1s on stone traffic from the Mendip quarries and around the South-East. DBS's fleet of Class 67s are mainly used on passenger or standby duties for Arriva Trains Wales, Chiltern Railways, East Coast and ScotRail. Class 90s are hired to ScotRail for use on the sleeping car services but see little use on freight, whilst the fleet of Class 92s are mainly used on intermodal duties, including a limited number of overnight trains on High Speed 1.

DBS also operates a number of excursion trains.

Devon & Cornwall Railways (a subsidiary of British American Railway Services): DCRail specialises in short-term freight haulage contracts, mainly in the scrap, coal and aggregates markets, using its fleet of Class 56s. It also provides locomotives from its fleet of 31s or 56s for stock moves and has some contracts with Network Rail for moving On Track Machines or other equipment.

Direct Rail Services: DRS has built on its original nuclear flask traffic to operate a number of different services. The main flows are intermodal plus the provision of crews and locos to Network Rail for autumn Railhead

Treatment Trains. Its Class 47s and 57s are also used on excursion work. DRS has the most varied fleet of locomotives, with Class 20s, 37s, 47s, 57s and 66s working alongside a fleet of Class 68s that are currently being delivered. The company has 25 Class 68s on order as well as ten new Vossloh electric locos (Class 88s), that will also feature a small diesel engine.

DRS also operates a number of excursion trains.

Freightliner: Freightliner has two divisions: Intermodal operates container trains from the main Ports at Southampton, Felixstowe, Tilbury and Thamesport to major cities including London, Manchester, Leeds and Birmingham. The Heavy Haul division covers the movement of coal, cement, infrastructure and aggregates nationwide. Most services are worked by Class 66s, with Class 70s used on some of the heavier intermodal trains and some Heavy Haul flows, principally coal, cement and ballast trains. A small fleet of Class 86 and 90 electrics is used on intermodal trains on the Great Eastern and West Coast Main Lines, the Class 86s mainly being used in pairs on the WCML between Crewe and Coatbridge.

GB Railfreight: GBRf, owned by Eurotunnel, operates a mixture of traffic types, mainly using Class 66s together with a small fleet of Class 73s on infrastructure duties in the South-East. A growing fleet of Class 92s is also used on some intermodal flows to/from Dollands Moor. Traffic includes coal, intermodal, biomass and gypsum as well as infrastructure services for Network Rail and London Underground.

GBRf also operates some excursion trains, including those using the preserved Class 201 "Hastings" DEMU.

West Coast Railway Company: WCRC has a freight licence but doesn't operate any freight as such – only empty stock movements. Its fleet of 47s, supplemented by a smaller number of 33s, 37s and 57s, is used on excursion work nationwide, including the prestigious Royal Scotsman.

In addition a number of other companies operate infrastructure trains, mainly formed of On-Track Machines. These include Balfour Beatty Rail Infrastructure Services, Swietelsky Babcock Rail, Volker Rail and South West Trains.

INTRODUCTION

SCOPE

This section contains details of all locomotives which can run on Britain's national railway network, plus those of Eurotunnel. Locomotives which are owned by, for example, DB Schenker and Freightliner which have been withdrawn from service and awaiting disposal are listed in the main part of the book. Locos which are awaiting disposal at scrapyards are listed in the "Locomotives Awaiting Disposal" section.

Only preserved locomotives which are currently certified for use on the National Rail network are included. Others, which may still be Network Rail registered but not at present certified for use, are not included, but will be found in the Platform 5 book, "Preserved Locomotives of British Railways".

CLASSIFICATION

Locomotive classes are listed in numerical order of class. Principal details and dimensions are quoted for each class in metric and/or imperial units as considered appropriate bearing in mind common UK usage.

All dimensions and weights are quoted for locomotives in an "as new" condition with all necessary supplies (eg oil, water and sand) on board. Dimensions are quoted in the order length x width. Lengths quoted are over buffers or couplers as appropriate. All widths quoted are maxima. Where two different wheel diameter dimensions are shown, the first refers to powered wheels and the second refers to non-powered wheels. All weights are shown as metric tonnes (t = tonnes).

LAYOUT OF INFORMATION

Locomotives are listed in numerical order. Where numbers actually carried are different from those officially allocated, these are noted in class headings where appropriate. Where locomotives have been recently renumbered, the most immediate previous number is shown in parentheses. Each locomotive entry is laid out as in the following example:

RSL No.	Detail	Livery	Owner	Pool		Allocn.	Name
60007	+*	**DB**	DB	WCBT		TO	The Spirit of Tom Kendell

Detail Differences. Only detail differences which currently affect the areas and types of train which locomotives may work are shown. All other detail differences are excluded. Where such differences occur within a class or part class, they are shown in the "Detail" column alongside the individual locomotive number.

ABBREVIATIONS

Standard abbreviations used in this book are:

a	Train air brake equipment only.
b	Drophead buckeye couplers.
c	Scharfenberg couplers.
d	Fitted with retractable Dellner couplers.
e	European Railway Traffic Management System (ERTMS) signalling equipment fitted.
i	Fitted with Tightlock couplers
k	Fitted with Swinghead Automatic "buckeye" combination couplers.
p	Train air, vacuum and electro-pneumatic brakes.
r	Radio Electric Token Block signalling equipment fitted.
s	Slow Speed Control equipment.
t	tonnes
v	Train vacuum brake only.
x	Train air and vacuum brakes ("Dual brakes").
+	Additional fuel tank capacity.
§	Sandite laying equipment.

In all cases use of the above abbreviations indicates the equipment indicated is normally operable. Meaning of non-standard abbreviations and symbols is detailed in individual class headings.

Codes: Codes are used to denote the livery, owner, pool and depot of each locomotive. Details of these will be found in section 7 of this book.
(S) denotes that the locomotive is currently stored.

Names: Only names carried with official sanction are listed. Names are shown in UPPER/lower case characters as actually shown on the name carried on the locomotive.

GENERAL INFORMATION

CLASSIFICATION AND NUMBERING

All locomotives are classified and allocated numbers by the Rolling Stock Library under the TOPS numbering system, introduced in 1972. This comprises a two-digit class number followed by a three-digit serial number. Where the actual number carried by a locomotive differs from the allocated number, or where an additional number is carried to the allocated number, this is shown by a note in the class heading.

For diesel locomotives, class numbers offer an indication of engine horsepower as shown in the table below.

Class No. Range	Engine hp
01–14	0–799
15–20	800–1000
21–31	1001–1499
32–39	1500–1999
40–54, 57	2000–2999
55–56, 58–70	3000+

For electric locomotives class numbers are allocated in ascending numerical order under the following scheme:

Class 71–80   Direct current and DC/diesel dual system locomotives.
Class 81 onwards   Alternating current and AC/DC dual system locos.

Numbers in the 89xxx series are allocated by the Rolling Stock Library to locomotives which have been deregistered but subsequently re-registered for use on the Network Rail network and whose original number has already been reused. 89xxx numbers are normally only carried inside locomotive cabs and are not carried externally in normal circumstances.

WHEEL ARRANGEMENT

For main line locomotives the number of driven axles on a bogie or frame is denoted by a letter (A = 1, B = 2, C = 3 etc) and the number of non-powered axles is denoted by a number. The use of the letter "o" after a letter indicates each axle is individually powered, whilst the "+" symbol indicates bogies are inter-coupled.

For shunting locomotives, the Whyte notation is used. In this notation the number of leading wheels are given, followed by the number of driving wheels and then the trailing wheels.

HAULAGE CAPABILITY OF DIESEL LOCOMOTIVES

The haulage capability of a diesel locomotive depends upon three basic factors:

1. Adhesive weight. The greater the weight on the driving wheels, the greater the adhesion and more tractive power can be applied before wheelslip occurs.

2. The characteristics of its transmission. To start a train the locomotive has to exert a pull at standstill. A direct drive diesel engine cannot do this, hence the need for transmission. This may be mechanical, hydraulic or electric. The present British Standard for locomotives is electric transmission. Here the diesel engine drives a generator or alternator and the current produced is fed to the traction motors. The force produced by each driven wheel depends on the current in its traction motor. In other words, the larger the current, the harder it pulls. As the locomotive speed increases, the current in the traction motor falls, hence the *Maximum Tractive Effort* is the maximum force at its wheels the locomotive can exert at a standstill. The electrical equipment cannot take such high currents for long without overheating. Hence the *Continuous Tractive Effort* is quoted which represents the current which the equipment can take continuously.

3. The power of its engine. Not all power reaches the rail, as electrical machines are approximately 90% efficient. As the electrical energy passes through two such machines (the generator or alternator and the traction motors), the *Power at Rail* is approximately 81% (90% of 90%) of the engine power, less a further amount used for auxiliary equipment such as radiator fans, traction motor blowers, air compressors, battery charging, cab heating, Electric Train Supply (ETS) etc. The power of the locomotive is proportional to the tractive effort times the speed. Hence when on full power there is a speed corresponding to the continuous tractive effort.

HAULAGE CAPABILITY OF ELECTRIC LOCOMOTIVES

Unlike a diesel locomotive, an electric locomotive does not develop its power on board and its performance is determined only by two factors, namely its weight and the characteristics of its electrical equipment. Whereas a diesel locomotive tends to be a constant power machine, the power of an electric locomotive varies considerably. Up to a certain speed it can produce virtually a constant tractive effort. Hence power rises with speed according to the formula given in section three above, until a maximum speed is reached at which tractive effort falls, such that the power also falls. Hence the power at the speed corresponding to the maximum tractive effort is lower than the maximum speed.

BRAKE FORCE

The brake force is a measure of the braking power of a locomotive. This is shown on the locomotive data panels so operating staff can ensure sufficient brake power is available on freight trains.

ELECTRIC TRAIN SUPPLY (ETS)

A number of locomotives are equipped to provide a supply of electricity to the train being hauled to power auxiliaries such as heating, cooling fans, air conditioning and kitchen equipment. ETS is provided from the locomotive by means of a separate alternator (except Class 33 locomotives, which have a DC generator). The ETS index of a locomotive is a measure of the electrical power available for train supply.

Similarly, most loco-hauled coaches also have an ETS index, which in this case is a measure of the power required to operate equipment mounted in the coach. The sum of the ETS indices of all the hauled vehicles in a train must not exceed the ETS index of the locomotive.

ETS is commonly (but incorrectly) known as ETH (Electric Train Heating), which is a throwback to the days before loco-hauled coaches were equipped with electrically powered auxiliary equipment other than for train heating.

ROUTE AVAILABILITY (RA)

This is a measure of a railway vehicle's axle load. The higher the axle load of a vehicle, the higher the RA number on a scale from 1 to 10. Each Network Rail route has a RA number and in general no vehicle with a higher RA number may travel on that route without special clearance.

MULTIPLE & PUSH-PULL WORKING

Multiple working between vehicles (ie two or more powered vehicles being driven from one cab) is facilitated by jumper cables connecting the vehicles. However, not all types are compatible with each other, and a number of different systems are in use, each system being incompatible with any other.

Association of American Railroads (AAR) System: Classes 59, 66, 67, 68 (some) and 70.
Blue Star Coupling Code: Classes 20, 25, 31, 33, 37 40 and 73.
DRS System: Classes 20/3, 37, 47 and 57.
Green Circle Coupling Code: Class 47 (not all equipped).
Orange Square Coupling Code: Class 50.
Red Diamond Coupling Code: Classes 56 and 58.
SR System: Classes 33/1, 73 and various electric multiple units.
Within Own Class only: Classes 43, 60, 68 (some).

Many locomotives use a time-division multiplex (TDM) system for push-pull and multiple working which utilises the existing RCH jumper cables fitted to coaching stock vehicles. Previously these cables had only been used to control train lighting and public address systems.

Class 47 locos 47701–47717 were equipped with an older non-standard TDM system.

1. DIESEL LOCOMOTIVES

CLASS 08   BR/ENGLISH ELECTRIC   0-6-0

Built: 1955–62 by BR at Crewe, Darlington, Derby Locomotive, Doncaster or Horwich Works.
Engine: English Electric 6KT of 298 kW (400 hp) at 680 rpm.
Main Generator: English Electric 801.
Traction Motors: Two English Electric 506.
Maximum Tractive Effort: 156 kN (35000 lbf).
Continuous Tractive Effort: 49 kN (11100 lbf) at 8.8 mph.
Power at Rail: 194 kW (260 hp).   **Train Brakes:** Air & vacuum.
Brake Force: 19 t.   **Dimensions:** 8.92 x 2.59 m.
Weight: 49.6–50.4 t.   **Wheel Diameter:** 1372 mm.
Design Speed: 20 mph.   **Maximum Speed:** 15 mph.
Fuel Capacity: 3037 litres.   **RA:** 5.
Train Supply: Not equipped.
Multiple Working: m Equipped for multiple working. All others not equipped.

† – Fitted with remote control equipment.

For shunting locomotives, instead of the two-letter depot code, actual locations at the time of publication are given.

Class 08s that don't have current Network Rail engineering acceptance and are considered to be "in industrial service" can be found in section 4 of this book.

08850 has acceptance for use between Battersby and Whitby only, for rescue purposes.

Non-standard liveries/numbering:

08480	Yellow with a red bodyside band. Carries number "TOTON No 1".
08616	Carries number 3783.
08696	Carries no number.
08701	Carries number "Tyne 100".
08721	As **B**, but with a black roof & "Express parcels" branding with red & yellow stripe.
08824	Carries number "IEMD01".
08899	Crimson lake.

Originally numbered in series D3000–D4192.

Class 08/0. Standard Design.

08405	a†	**E**	DB	WQAA	Dagenham Yard (S)
08410	a	**FB**	FW	EFSH	RVEL Derby
08417	a	**Y**	NR	QADD	RVEL Derby
08428	ak	**E**	DB	WQAA	Carlisle Yards (S)
08451		**B**	AM	ATLO	Manchester Longsight Depot
08454		**K**	AM	ATLO	Wolverhampton Oxley Depot
08472	a	**WA**	WA	RFSH	Edinburgh Craigentinny Depot
08480	a	**0**	DB	WQBA	Toton Depot (S)

▲ 08649 shunts two Greater Anglia Mark 3s at Knorr Bremse Rail Services' Wolverton site on 16/04/14.　　**John Pink**

▼ Harry Needle Railroad Company 08943 is seen at the Bombardier Transportation depot at Central Rivers on 08/10/13.　　**Paul Abell**

▲ BR Railfreight grey-liveried 20132 and 20118 are seen stabled at Derby on 13/09/14. **Robert Pritchard**

▼ Devon & Cornwall Railways green-liveried 31601 passes Shipton-by-Benningborough with a Darlington–York engineers train on 18/05/14.
Andrew Mason

▲ West Coast Railway Company-liveried 33029 passes Shrivenham with a train of empty coaching stock from Southall to Bristol on 26/07/14. **Jamie Squibbs**

▼ Newly restored to main line action, BR Blue-liveried 40145 passes Horbury Bridge, east of Healey Mills, with a 13.14 Carnforth–Castleton railtour on 06/06/14.

Andrew Wills

▲ In the latest DRS livery, 37423 runs off the Deepcar branch at Nunnery, Sheffield, with an 09.49 Doncaster West Yard–Derby test train on 01/07/14. 37667 was on the rear of the train.
Andrew Wills

▲ The Network Rail New Measurement Train HST, with power cars 43014/013, passes Cleghorn with a 12.07 Glasgow Central–Crewe on 15/04/14. **Robin Ralston**

▼ East Midlands Trains HST 43073/044 passes through the Mere Valley shortly after departure from Scarborough with the 17.03 Scarborough–London St Pancras on 09/08/14. **Andrew Mason**

▲ Riviera Trains-liveried 47843 leads the 06.58 Doncaster–Great Yarmouth GBRf charter near Syston on 24/08/14. **Louis Hurst**

▼ Back on the main line in 2014 was BR blue-liveried 50007, seen here double-heading the 08.59 Washwood Heath–Boston Docks steel train with Colas Rail 56105 at Hemington, near Castle Donington, on 17/05/14. **Paul Biggs**

▲ BR Maroon-liveried D1015 "Western Champion" rounds the curve at Marazion with an 05.00 Tame Bridge Parkway–Penzance railtour on 28/06/14. **Ron Westwater**

▼ Colas Rail 56105 passes Caverswall, near Blythe Bridge, with 6S96 13.15 Sinfin–Grangemouth empty tanks on 12/06/14. **Cliff Beeton**

▲ West Coast Railway Company-liveried 57601 passes Plean with the 14.30 Stirling–London Euston Statesman railtour on 17/08/13.   **Ian Lothian**

▼ Aggregate Industries-liveried 59001 passes Berkley, near Frome, with 6C76 14.40 Acton–Merehead stone empties on 13/06/13.   **Roger Geach**

08483	a	GL	FW	EFSH	RVEL Derby
08495	†	E	DB	WQBA	Crewe International Depot (S)
08500		E	DB	WQCA	Tees Yard (S)
08523		RS	RL	MRSO	Inverness Depot
08525		ST	EM	EMSL	Leeds Neville Hill Depot
08530		FL	P	DFLS	Southampton Maritime FLT
08531	a	FL	P	DFLS	Felixstowe FLT
08567	†	E	DB	WQBA	Crewe International Depot (S)
08571	a	WA	WA	HBSH	Bounds Green Depot
08575		FL	P	DHLT	LH Group, Barton-under-Needwood (S)
08578	†	E	DB	WQCA	Toton Depot (S)
08580		E	DB	WQCA	Bescot Yards (S)
08585		FL	P	DFLS	Felixstowe FLT
08593		E	DB	WQCA	Crewe International Depot (S)
08596	a†	WA	WA	HBSH	Bounds Green Depot
08605	†	E	DB	WQAA	Toton Depot (S)
08611		V	AM	ATLO	Manchester Longsight Depot
08615		WA	WA	RFSH	Edinburgh Craigentinny Depot
08616		LM	LM	EJLO	Birmingham Tyseley Depot
08617		K	AM	ATLO	Wembley Depot
08623		DB	DB	WSSC	Hoo Junction Yards
08624		FL	P	DFLS	Trafford Park FLT
08630		E	DB	WQCA	Toton Yards (S)
08632	†	DB	DB	WQAA	Mossend Yards (S)
08633	†	E	DB	WQAA	Toton Depot (S)
08641		B	FW	EFSH	Penzance Long Rock Depot
08644		B	FW	EFSH	Plymouth Laira Depot
08645		DG	FW	EFSH	Plymouth Laira Depot
08653		E	DB	WQCA	Toton Yards (S)
08663	a	FB	FW	EFSH	Old Oak Common HST Depot
08669	a	WA	WA	RFSH	Wabtec Rail, Doncaster Works
08676	†	E	DB	WQAA	Toton Depot (S)
08690		ST	EM	EMSL	Leeds Neville Hill Depot
08691		FL	FL	DFLS	Southampton Maritime FLT
08696	a	G	AM	ATLO	Glasgow Polmadie Depot
08697	a	B	EM	QADD	RVEL Derby
08701	a†	RX	DB	WQCA	Toton Yards (S)
08703	a	E	DB	WSSC	Margam Yard
08706	†	E	DB	WQCA	Crewe International Depot (S)
08709		E	DB	WQCA	Bescot Yards (S)
08711	k	RX	DB	WQCA	Tees Yard (S)
08714		E	DB	WQAA	Crewe International Depot (S)
08721		0	AM	ATLO	Liverpool Edge Hill Depot
08724		WA	WA	HBSH	Wabtec Rail, Doncaster Works
08735	†	E	DB	WQCA	Eastleigh Yards (S)
08737	a†	E	DB	WQBA	Crewe International Depot (S)
08738	m	ECR	DB	WQCA	Toton Yards (S)
08742	†	RX	DB	WQAA	Millerhill Yard (S)
08752	†	E	DB	WSSC	Tyne Yard
08754		B	RL	MRSO	Norwich Crown Point Depot
08757	†	RG	DB	WQBA	Crewe International Depot (S)

08782	a†	CU	DB	WQAA	Doncaster Yards (S)
08784	†	E	DB	WQBA	Toton Depot (S)
08785	a	FL	P	DFLS	LH Group, Barton-under-Needwood
08788		K	RL	MRSO	Inverness Depot
08790		B	AM	ATLO	Eastleigh Works
08795		K	FW	EFSH	Swansea Landore Depot
08799	a	E	DB	WQAA	Westbury Yards (S)
08802	†	E	DB	WQAA	Toton Depot (S)
08804	†	E	DB	WQBA	Crewe International Depot (S)
08805		B	LM	EJLO	Birmingham Soho Depot
08822		FB	FW	EFSH	Bristol St Philip's Marsh Depot
08824	ak	K	DB	WQAA	Crewe International Depot (S)
08836		FB	FW	EFSH	Old Oak Common HST Depot
08847		CD	RL	MRSO	RMS Locotec, Washwood Heath
08850		B	NY	MBDL	Grosmont Depot
08853	a	WA	WA	RFSH	Wabtec Rail, Doncaster Works
08865		E	DB	WQBA	Crewe International Depot (S)
08874		SL	RL	MRSO	Norwich Crown Point Depot
08877		DG	DB	WQCA	Wigan Springs Branch Depot
08879	†	E	DB	WQAA	Hinksey Yard (S)
08886		E	DB	WQCA	Crewe International Depot (S)
08887	a	B	AM	ATLO	Wembley Depot
08888	†	E	DB	WQAA	Didcot Yards (S)
08891		FL	P	DHLT	LH Group, Barton-under-Needwood (S)
08899		O	EM	EMSL	Derby Etches Park Depot
08904		E	DB	WQAA	Eastleigh Yards (S)
08907		DB	DB	WQAA	Bescot Yards (S)
08908		ST	EM	EMSL	Leeds Neville Hill Depot
08922		DG	DB	WQBA	Toton Depot (S)
08925		G	GB	GBWM	March Whitemoor Yard
08934	a	VP	GB	GBWM	Cardiff Tidal Steelworks
08939	m	ECR	DB	WQCA	Toton Yards (S)
08948	c	EP	EU	GPSS	Temple Mills Depot
08950		ST	EM	EMSL	Leeds Neville Hill Depot
08954		B	AM	ATLO	Glasgow Polmadie Depot

Class 08/9. Reduced height cab. Converted 1985–87 by BR at Landore.

08993		E	DB	WQBA	Axiom Rail, Stoke-on-Trent Works (S)
08994	a	E	DB	WQCA	Toton Depot (S)
08995	a	E	DB	WQBA	Crewe International Depot (S)

CLASS 09   BR/ENGLISH ELECTRIC   0-6-0

Built: 1959–62 by BR at Darlington or Horwich Works.
Engine: English Electric 6KT of 298 kW (400 hp) at 680 rpm.
Main Generator: English Electric 801.
Traction Motors: English Electric 506.
Maximum Tractive Effort: 111 kN (25000 lbf).
Continuous Tractive Effort: 39 kN (8800 lbf) at 11.6 mph.

Power at Rail: 201 kW (269 hp).	**Train Brakes:** Air & vacuum.
Brake Force: 19 t.	**Dimensions:** 8.92 x 2.59 m.
Weight: 49 t.	**Wheel Diameter:** 1372 mm.
Design Speed: 27 mph.	**Maximum Speed:** 27 mph.
Fuel Capacity: 3037 litres.	**RA:** 5.
Train Supply: Not equipped.	**Multiple Working:** Not equipped.

Class 09s that don't have current Network Rail engineering acceptance and are considered to be "in industrial service" can be found in section 4 of this book.

Class 09/0 were originally numbered D3665–D3671, D3719–D3721, D4099–D4114.

Class 09/0. Built as Class 09.

09002	**G**	GB	GBWM	March Whitemoor Yard
09006	**E**	DB	WQCA	Toton Depot (S)
09009	**G**	GB	GBWM	Dagenham Yard
09026 a	**G**	SN	HWSU	Brighton Lovers Walk Depot

Class 09/1. Converted from Class 08. 110 V electrical equipment.
Converted: 1992–1993 by RFS Industries, Kilnhurst.

09106 (08759)	**DB**	DB	WSSC	Warrington Yards

Class 09/2. Converted from Class 08. 90 V electrical equipment.
Converted: 1992 by RFS Industries, Kilnhurst.

09201 (08421) ak†	**DG**	DB	WQAA	Toton Depot (S)

Class 08 and Class 09 names:

08451	M.A. SMITH		08782	CASTLETON WORKS
08483	DUSTY Driver David Miller		08790	Steve Purser
08495	NOEL KIRTON OBE		08799	FRED
08525	DUNCAN BEDFORD		08805	CONCORDE
08585	Vicky		08822	John
08616	TYSELEY 100		08874	Catherine
08630	BOB BROWN		08899	Midland Counties Railway
08645	Mike Baggott			175 1839–2014
08669	Bob Machin		08908	IVAN STEPHENSON
08690	DAVID THIRKILL		08950	DAVID LIGHTFOOT
08691	Terri		09026	Cedric Wares
08721	DOWNHILL C.S.			

CLASS 20   ENGLISH ELECTRIC   Bo-Bo

Built: 1957–68 by English Electric at Vulcan Foundry, Newton-le-Willows or by Robert Stephenson & Hawthorns at Darlington.
Engine: English Electric 8SVT Mk II of 746 kW (1000 hp) at 850 rpm.
Main Generator: English Electric 819/3C.
Traction Motors: English Electric 526/5D or 526/8D.
Maximum Tractive Effort: 187 kN (42000 lbf).
Continuous Tractive Effort: 111 kN (25000 lbf) at 11 mph.
Power at Rail: 574 kW (770 hp).   **Train Brakes:** Air & vacuum.
Brake Force: 35 t.   **Dimensions:** 14.25 x 2.67 m.
Weight: 73.4–73.5 t.   **Wheel Diameter:** 1092 mm.
Design Speed: 75 mph.   **Maximum Speed:** 75 mph.
Fuel Capacity: 1727 litres.   **RA:** 5.
Train Supply: Not equipped.   **Multiple Working:** Blue Star.

Class 20s that don't have current Network Rail engineering acceptance and are considered to be "in industrial service" can be found in section 4 of this book.

Originally numbered in series D8007–D8190, D8315–D8325.

Non-standard liveries/numbering:

20088 RFS grey (carries No. 2017).
20227 White, red & blue with London Underground roundels.

Class 20/0. Standard Design.

20016	**B**	HN	HNRS	LM (S)	
20081	**B**	HN	HNRS	LM (S)	
20088	**0**	HN	HNRS	LM (S)	
20092	**U**	HN	HNRS	LM (S)	
20096	**B**	HN	GBEE	BH	
20107	**B**	HN	GBEE	BH	
20118	**FO**	HN	GBEE	BH	Saltburn-by-the-Sea
20132	**FO**	HN	GBEE	BH	Barrow Hill Depot
20142	**BB**	20	MOLO	SK	
20189	**BB**	20	MOLO	SK	
20205	**B**	2L	MBDL	SK	
20227	**0**	2L	GBEE	SK	

Class 20/3. Direct Rail Services refurbished locos. Details as Class 20/0 except:

Refurbished: 15 locomotives were refurbished 1995–96 by Brush Traction at Loughborough (20301–305) or 1997–98 by RFS(E) at Doncaster (20306–315). Disc indicators or headcode panels removed.
Train Brakes: Air.   **Maximum Speed:** 60 mph (+ 75 mph).
Weight: 73 t (+ 76 t).   **Fuel Capacity:** 2909 (+ 4909 litres).
Brake Force: 35 t (+ 31 t).   **RA:** 5 (+ 6).
Multiple Working: DRS system.

20301	(20047)	r	**DS**	DR	XHSS	BH (S)	Max Joule 1958–1999
20302	(20084)	r	**DS**	DR	XHNC	KM	
20303	(20127)	r	**DS**	DR	XHNC	KM	
20304	(20120)	r	**DS**	DR	XHNC	KM	

20305	(20095)	r	**DS**	DR	XHNC	KM	Gresty Bridge
20308	(20187)	r+	**DS**	DR	XHNC	KM	
20309	(20075)	r+	**DS**	DR	XHNC	KM	
20311	(20102)	r+	**HN**	HN	GBEE	BH	
20312	(20042)	r+	**DS**	DR	XHNC	KM	
20314	(20117)	r+	**HN**	HN	GBEE	BH	

Class 20/9. Harry Needle Railroad Company (former Hunslet-Barclay/DRS) locos. Details as Class 20/0 except:

Refurbished: 1989 by Hunslet-Barclay at Kilmarnock.
Train Brakes: Air.   **Fuel Capacity:** 1727 (+ 4727) litres.
RA: 5 (+ 6).

20901	(20101)		**GB**	HN	GBEE	BH	
20903	(20083)	+	**DR**	HN	HNRS	BO (S)	
20904	(20041)	+	**DR**	HN	HNRS	BO (S)	
20905	(20225)	+	**GB**	HN	GBEE	BH	

CLASS 25   BR/BEYER PEACOCK/SULZER   Bo-Bo

Built: 1965 by Beyer Peacock at Gorton.
Engine: Sulzer 6LDA28-B of 930 kW (1250 hp) at 750 rpm.
Main Generator: AEI RTB15656.   **Traction Motors:** AEI 253AY.
Maximum Tractive Effort: 200 kN (45000 lbf).
Continuous Tractive Effort: 93 kN (20800 lbf) at 17.1 mph.
Power at Rail: 708 kW (949 hp).   **Train Brakes:** Air & vacuum.
Brake Force: 38 t.   **Dimensions:** 15.39 x 2.73 m.
Weight: 71.5 t.   **Wheel Diameter:** 1143 mm.
Design Speed: 90 mph.   **Maximum Speed:** 60 mph.
Fuel Capacity: 2270 litres.   **RA:** 5.
Train Supply: Not equipped.   **Multiple Working:** Blue Star.

Original number is D7628, which the loco currently carries.

Only certified for use on Network Rail metals between Whitby and Battersby, as an extension of North Yorkshire Moors Railway services.

| 25278 | **GG** | NY | MBDL | NY | SYBILLA |

CLASS 31   BRUSH/ENGLISH ELECTRIC   A1A-A1A

Built: 1958–62 by Brush Traction at Loughborough.
Engine: English Electric 12SVT of 1100 kW (1470 hp) at 850 rpm.
Main Generator: Brush TG160-48.   **Traction Motors:** Brush TM73-68.
Maximum Tractive Effort: 160 kN (35900 lbf).
Continuous Tractive Effort: 83 kN (18700 lbf) at 23.5 mph.
Power at Rail: 872 kW (1170 hp).   **Train Brakes:** Air & vacuum.
Brake Force: 49 t.   **Dimensions:** 17.30 x 2.67 m.
Weight: 106.7–111 t.   **Wheel Diameter:** 1092/1003 mm.
Design Speed: 90 mph.   **Maximum Speed:** 90 mph.
Fuel Capacity: 2409 litres.   **RA:** 5 or 6.
Train Supply: Not equipped.   **Multiple Working:** Blue Star.

Originally numbered D5520–D5699, D5800–D5862 (not in order).

Non-standard numbering: 31190 Also carries number D5613.

Class 31/1. Standard Design. RA: 5.

31105	**Y**	NR	QADD	ZA	
31106 a	**B**	HJ	RVLO	ZA	
31128	**B**	NS	NRLO	NY	CHARYBDIS
31190	**G**	BA	HTLX	WH	
31233 a	**Y**	NR	QADD	ZA	
31285	**Y**	NR	QADD	ZA	

Class 31/4. Electric Train Supply equipment. RA: 6.
Train Supply: Electric, index 66.

31452	**DC**	BA	HTLX	ZA	
31454	**IC**	BA	HTLX	WH (S)	
31459	**K**	BA	RVLO	ZA (S)	CERBERUS
31465	**Y**	NR	QADD	ZA	
31468	**FR**	BA	RVLO	WO (S)	HYDRA

Class 31/6. ETS through wiring and controls. RA: 5.

31601	(31186)	**DC**	BA	HTLX	WH
31602	(31191)	**Y**	BA	HTLX	WO (S)

CLASS 33   BRCW/SULZER   Bo-Bo

Built: 1960–62 by the Birmingham Railway Carriage & Wagon Company at Smethwick.
Engine: Sulzer 8LDA28 of 1160 kW (1550 hp) at 750 rpm.
Main Generator: Crompton Parkinson CG391B1.
Traction Motors: Crompton Parkinson C171C2.
Maximum Tractive Effort: 200 kN (45000 lbf).
Continuous Tractive Effort: 116 kN (26000 lbf) at 17.5 mph.
Power at Rail: 906 kW (1215 hp).   **Train Brakes:** Air & vacuum.
Brake Force: 35 t.   **Dimensions:** 15.47 x 2.82 (2.64 m 33/2).
Weight: 76-78 t.   **Wheel Diameter:** 1092 mm.
Design Speed: 85 mph.   **Maximum Speed:** 85 mph.
Fuel Capacity: 3410 litres.   **RA:** 6.
Train Supply: Electric, index 48 (750 V DC only).
Multiple Working: Blue Star.

Originally numbered in series D6500–D6597 but not in order.

Non-standard numbering: 33012 Carries number D6515.

Class 33/0. Standard Design.

33012	**G**	71	MBDL	Swanage Rly	Lt Jenny Lewis RN
33025	**WC**	WC	AWCX	SH (S)	Glen Falloch
33029	**WC**	WC	AWCA	CS	
33030	**DR**	WC	AWCX	CS (S)	

Class 33/2. Built to former Loading Gauge of Tonbridge–Battle Line.
Equipped with slow speed control.

33207	**WC**	WC	AWCA	CS	Jim Martin

CLASS 37   ENGLISH ELECTRIC   Co-Co

Built: 1960–66 by English Electric at Vulcan Foundry, Newton-le-Willows or by Robert Stephenson & Hawthorns at Darlington.
Engine: English Electric 12CSVT of 1300 kW (1750 hp) at 850 rpm.
Main Generator: English Electric 822/10G.
Traction Motors: English Electric 538/A.
Maximum Tractive Effort: 247 kN (55500 lbf).
Continuous Tractive Effort: 156 kN (35000 lbf) at 13.6 mph.

Power at Rail: 932 kW (1250 hp).	**Train Brakes:** Air & vacuum.
Brake Force: 50 t.	**Dimensions:** 18.75 x 2.74 m.
Weight: 102.8–108.4 t.	**Wheel Diameter:** 1092 mm.
Design Speed: 90 mph.	**Maximum Speed:** 80 mph.
Fuel Capacity: 4046 (+ 7683) litres.	**RA:** 5 (§ 6).

Train Supply: Not equipped.
Multiple Working: Blue Star († DRS system).

Originally numbered D6600–D6608, D6700–D6999 (not in order).

Class 37/0. Standard Design. Details as above.

37038	a†	**DR**	DR	XHSS	LB (S)
37059	ar+†	**DI**	DR	XHNC	KM
37069	ar+†	**DS**	DR	XHSS	LB (S)
37116	+	**B**	CS	COTS	WH (S)
37165	a+	**CE**	WC	AWCX	CS (S)
37175	a	**CS**	CS	COTS	RU
37194	a+†	**DS**	DR	XHNC	KM
37198	+	**Y**	NR	MBDL	GCR (S) CHIEF ENGINEER
37214		**WC**	WC	AWCX	CS (S)
37218	ar+†	**DI**	DR	XHNC	KM
37219		**CS**	CS	COTS	RU
37259	ar†	**DS**	DR	XHNC	KM

Class 37/4. Refurbished with electric train supply equipment. Main generator replaced by alternator. Regeared (CP7) bogies. Details as Class 37/0 except:
Main Alternator: Brush BA1005A.   **Power At Rail:** 935 kW (1254 hp).
Traction Motors: English Electric 538/5A.
Maximum Tractive Effort: 256 kN (57440 lbf).
Continuous Tractive Effort: 184 kN (41250 lbf) at 11.4 mph.

Weight: 107 t.	**Design Speed:** 80 mph.

Fuel Capacity: 7683 litres.
Train Supply: Electric, index 30.

37401	ar	**BL**	DR	XHHP	ZA (S)	Mary Queen of Scots
37402	a	**DS**	DR	XHAC	KM	Stephen Middlemore 23.12.1954–8.6.2013
37405		**DS**	DR	XHAC	KM	
37409	ar†	**DS**	DR	XHAC	KM	Lord Hinton
37419	ar	**DS**	DR	XHAC	KM	Carl Haviland 1954–2012
37421		**CS**	CS	COTS	RU	
37422	ar	**DS**	DR	XHHP	BH (S)	
37423	ar†	**DI**	DR	XHAC	KM	Spirit of the Lakes
37425	ar	**DS**	DR	XHAC	KM	Sir Robert McAlpine/Concrete Bob

Class 37/5. Refurbished without train supply equipment. Main generator replaced by alternator. Regeared (CP7) bogies. Details as Class 37/4 except:
Power At Rail: 932 kW (1250 hp).
Maximum Tractive Effort: 248 kN (55590 lbf).
Continuous Tractive Effort: 184 kN (41250 lbf) at 11.4 mph.
Weight: 106.1–110.0 t.

37503	r§	**E**	DR	XHHP	BH (S)
37510	a	**DS**	DR	XHSS	BH (S)
37516	s	**WC**	WC	AWCA	CS	Loch Laidon
37517	as	**LH**	WC	AWCX	CS (S)
37518	ar	**IC**	WC	AWCA	CS	Fort William/An Gearasdan
37521	r§	**E**	DR	XHHP	BH (S)	English China Clays

Class 37/6. Originally refurbished for Nightstar services. Main generator replaced by alternator. UIC jumpers. Details as Class 37/5 except:
Maximum Speed: 90 mph.   **Train Brake:** Air.
Train Supply: Not equipped, but electric through wired.
Multiple Working: DRS system.

37601	a	**DS**	DR	XHNC	KM	Class 37-'Fifty'
37602	ar	**DS**	DR	XHNC	KM
37603	a	**DS**	DR	XHNC	KM
37604	a	**DS**	DR	XHNC	KM
37605	ar	**DS**	DR	XHNC	KM
37606	a	**DS**	DR	XHNC	KM
37607	ar	**DS**	DR	XHNC	KM
37608	ar	**DS**	DR	XHNC	KM
37609	a	**DI**	DR	XHNC	KM
37610	ar	**DS**	DR	XHNC	KM	T.S.(Ted) Cassady 14.5.61–6.4.08
37611	a	**DS**	DR	XHNC	KM
37612	a	**DS**	DR	XHNC	KM

Class 37/5 continued.

37667	arst	**DS**	DR	XHNC	KM
37668	s	**WC**	WC	AWCA	CS
37669	r	**WC**	WC	AWCA	CS
37670	r	**DB**	DR	XHSS	ZA (S)
37676	a	**WC**	WC	AWCA	CS	Loch Rannoch
37682	ar	**DS**	DR	XHNC	KM
37685	a	**WC**	WC	AWCA	CS	Loch Arkaig
37688	ar†	**DS**	DR	XHNC	KM	Kingmoor TMD
37696	as	**F**	DR	XHHP	ZA (S)

Class 37/7. Refurbished locos. Main generator replaced by alternator. Regeared (CP7) bogies. Ballast weights added. Details as Class 37/5 except:
Main Alternator: GEC G564AZ (37796–803) Brush BA1005A (others).
Maximum Tractive Effort: 276 kN (62000 lbf).
Weight: 120 t.   **RA:** 7.

37703		**DR**	DR	XHHP	Bo'ness
37706		**WC**	WC	AWCA	CS
37710		**LH**	WC	AWCX	CS (S)

37712 a	**WC**	WC	AWCX	CS (S)	
37714	**DR**	DR	XHHP	BH (S)	
37716	**DI**	DR	XHHP	ZA (S)	
37718	**GIF**	DR	XHHP	ZA (S)	
37800	**GIF**	EP	EPUK	WH (S)	
37884	**EX**	EP	EPUK	WH	

Class 97/3. Class 37s refurbished for Network Rail for use on the Cambrian Lines which are signalled by ERTMS. Details as Class 37/0.

97301 (37100) e	**Y**	NR	QETS	ZA	
97302 (37170) e	**Y**	NR	QETS	ZA	
97303 (37178) e	**Y**	NR	QETS	ZA	
97304 (37217) e	**Y**	NR	QETS	ZA	John Tiley

CLASS 40   ENGLISH ELECTRIC   1Co-Co1

Built: 1958–62 by English Electric at Vulcan Foundry, Newton-le-Willows.
Engine: English Electric 16SVT Mk2 of 1490 kW (2000 hp) at 850 rpm.
Main Generator: English Electric 822/4C.
Traction Motors: English Electric 526/5D or EE526/7D.
Maximum Tractive Effort: 231 kN (52000 lbf).
Continuous Tractive Effort: 137 kN (30900 lbf) at 18.8 mph.

Power at Rail: 1160 kW (1550 hp).	**Train Brakes:** Air & vacuum.	
Brake Force: 51 t.	**Dimensions:** 21.18 x 2.78 m.	
Weight: 132 t.	**Wheel Diameter:** 914/1143 mm.	
Design Speed: 90 mph.	**Maximum Speed:** 90 mph.	
Fuel Capacity: 3250 litres.	**RA:** 6.	
Train Supply: Steam.	**Multiple Working:** Blue Star.	

Originally numbered D345. Currently carries No. 345.

40145	**B**	40	ELRD	BQ	

CLASS 43   BREL/PAXMAN   Bo-Bo

Built: 1975–82 by BREL at Crewe Works.
Engine: MTU 16V4000R41R of 1680kW (2250 hp) at 1500 rpm.
(* Paxman 12VP185 of 1565 kW (2100 hp) at 1500 rpm.)
Main Alternator: Brush BA1001B.
Traction Motors: Brush TMH68–46 or GEC G417AZ (43124–152), frame mounted.
Maximum Tractive Effort: 80 kN (17980 lbf).
Continuous Tractive Effort: 46 kN (10340 lbf) at 64.5 mph.

Power at Rail: 1320 kW (1770 hp).	**Train Brakes:** Air.	
Brake Force: 35 t.	**Dimensions:** 17.79 x 2.74 m.	
Weight: 70.25–75.0 t.	**Wheel Diameter:** 1020 mm.	
Design Speed: 125 mph.	**Maximum Speed:** 125 mph.	
Fuel Capacity: 4500 litres.	**RA:** 5.	
Train Supply: Three-phase electric.		

Multiple Working: Within class, jumpers at non-driving end only.

† Buffer fitted.

43013, 43014 & 43062 are fitted with measuring apparatus & front-end cameras.

Advertising livery: 43163 – Visit Plymouth (blue).

43002	FB	A	EFPC	LA	
43003	FB	A	EFPC	LA	ISAMBARD KINGDOM BRUNEL
43004	FB	A	EFPC	LA	First for the future/
					First ar gyfer y dyfodol
43005	FB	A	EFPC	LA	
43009	FB	A	EFPC	LA	
43010	FB	A	EFPC	LA	
43012	FB	A	EFPC	LA	
43013 †	Y	P	QCAR	EC	
43014 †	Y	P	QCAR	EC	The Railway Observer
43015	FB	A	EFPC	LA	
43016	FB	A	EFPC	LA	
43017	FB	A	EFPC	LA	Hannahs discoverhannahs.org
43018	FB	A	EFPC	LA	
43020	FB	A	EFPC	LA	MTU Power. Passion. Partnership
43021	FB	A	EFPC	LA	David Austin – Cartoonist
43022	FB	A	EFPC	LA	
43023	FB	A	EFPC	LA	
43024	FB	A	EFPC	LA	Great Western Society 1961–2011
					Didcot Railway Centre
43025	FB	A	EFPC	LA	IRO The Institution of Railway Operators
					2000–2010 TEN YEARS
					PROMOTING OPERATIONAL EXCELLENCE
43026	FB	A	EFPC	LA	
43027	FB	A	EFPC	LA	Glorious Devon
43028	FB	A	EFPC	LA	
43029	FB	A	EFPC	LA	
43030	FB	A	EFPC	LA	Christian Lewis Trust
43031	FB	A	EFPC	LA	
43032	FB	A	EFPC	LA	
43033	FB	A	EFPC	LA	Driver Brian Cooper
					15 June 1947–5 October 1999
43034	FB	A	EFPC	LA	TravelWatch SouthWest
43035	FB	A	EFPC	LA	
43036	FB	A	EFPC	LA	
43037	FB	A	EFPC	LA	PENYDARREN
43040	FB	A	EFPC	LA	Bristol St. Philip's Marsh
43041	FB	A	EFPC	LE	Meningitis Trust Support for Life
43042	FB	A	EFPC	LE	
43043 *	ST	P	EMPC	NL	
43044 *	ST	P	EMPC	NL	
43045 *	ST	P	EMPC	NL	
43046 *	ST	P	EMPC	NL	
43047 *	ST	P	EMPC	NL	
43048 *	ST	P	EMPC	NL	T.C.B. Miller MBE
43049 *	ST	P	EMPC	NL	Neville Hill
43050 *	ST	P	EMPC	NL	
43052 *	ST	P	EMPC	NL	
43053	FB	P	EFPC	LE	University of Worcester

43054	*	**ST**	P	EMPC	NL	
43055	*	**ST**	P	EMPC	NL	The Sheffield Star 125 Years
43056		**FB**	P	EFPC	LE	The Royal British Legion
43058	*	**ST**	P	EMPC	NL	
43059	*	**ST**	P	EMPC	NL	
43060	*	**ST**	P	EMPC	NL	
43061	*	**ST**	P	EMPC	NL	
43062		**Y**	P	QCAR	EC	John Armitt
43063		**FB**	P	EFPC	LE	
43064	*	**ST**	P	EMPC	NL	
43066	*	**ST**	P	EMPC	NL	
43069		**FB**	P	EFPC	LE	
43070		**FB**	P	EFPC	LE	The Corps of Royal Electrical and Mechanical Engineers
43071		**FB**	P	EFPC	LE	
43073	*	**ST**	P	EMPC	NL	
43075	*	**ST**	P	EMPC	NL	
43076	*	**ST**	P	EMPC	NL	IN SUPPORT OF HELP for HEROES
43078		**FB**	P	EFPC	LE	
43079		**FB**	P	EFPC	LE	
43081	*	**ST**	P	EMPC	NL	
43082	*	**ST**	P	EMPC	NL	RAILWAY children – THE VOICE FOR STREET CHILDREN WORLDWIDE
43083	*	**ST**	P	EMPC	NL	
43086		**FB**	P	EFPC	OO	
43087		**FB**	P	EFPC	OO	11 Explosive Ordnance Disposal Regiment Royal Logistic Corps
43088		**FB**	P	EFPC	OO	
43089	*	**ST**	P	EMPC	NL	
43091		**FB**	P	EFPC	OO	
43092		**FB**	FG	EFPC	OO	
43093		**FB**	FG	EFPC	OO	
43094		**FB**	FG	EFPC	OO	
43097		**FB**	FG	EFPC	OO	Environment Agency
43098		**FB**	FG	EFPC	OO	
43122		**FB**	FG	EFPC	OO	
43124		**FB**	A	EFPC	LE	
43125		**FB**	A	EFPC	LE	
43126		**FB**	A	EFPC	LE	
43127		**FB**	A	EFPC	LE	Sir Peter Parker 1924–2002 Cotswold Line 150
43128		**FB**	A	EFPC	LE	
43129		**FB**	A	EFPC	LE	
43130		**FB**	A	EFPC	LE	
43131		**FB**	A	EFPC	LE	
43132		**FB**	A	EFPC	LE	We Save the Children – Will You?
43133		**FB**	A	EFPC	LE	
43134		**FB**	A	EFPC	LE	
43135		**FB**	A	EFPC	LE	
43136		**FB**	A	EFPC	LE	
43137		**FB**	A	EFPC	LE	Newton Abbot 150

43138	**FB**	A	EFPC	LE	
43139	**FB**	A	EFPC	LE	Driver Stan Martin
					25 June 1950 – 6 November 2004
43140	**FB**	A	EFPC	LE	Landore Diesel Depot
					1963 Celebrating 50 years 2013/
					Depo Diesel Glandŵr
					1963 Dathlu 50 Mlynedd 2013
43141	**FB**	A	EFPC	LE	
43142	**FB**	A	EFPC	LE	Reading Panel Signal Box 1965–2010
43143	**FB**	A	EFPC	LE	Stroud 700
43144	**FB**	A	EFPC	LE	
43145	**FB**	A	EFPC	LE	
43146	**FB**	A	EFPC	LE	
43147	**FB**	A	EFPC	LE	Royal Marines
					Celebrating 350 Years
43148	**FB**	A	EFPC	LE	
43149	**FB**	A	EFPC	LE	University of Plymouth
43150	**FB**	A	EFPC	LE	
43151	**FB**	A	EFPC	LE	
43152	**FB**	A	EFPC	LE	
43153	**FB**	FG	EFPC	OO	
43154	**FB**	FG	EFPC	OO	
43155	**FB**	FG	EFPC	OO	The Red Arrows
					50 Seasons of Excellence
43156	**FB**	P	EFPC	OO	Dartington International Summer School
43158	**FB**	FG	EFPC	OO	
43159	**FB**	P	EFPC	OO	
43160	**FB**	P	EFPC	OO	Sir Moir Lockhead OBE
43161	**FB**	P	EFPC	OO	
43162	**FB**	P	EFPC	OO	
43163	**AL**	A	EFPC	OO	
43164	**FB**	A	EFPC	OO	
43165	**FB**	A	EFPC	OO	Prince Michael of Kent
43168	**FB**	A	EFPC	OO	
43169	**FB**	A	EFPC	OO	THE NATIONAL TRUST
43170	**FB**	A	EFPC	OO	
43171	**FB**	A	EFPC	OO	
43172	**FB**	A	EFPC	OO	
43174	**FB**	A	EFPC	OO	
43175	**FB**	A	EFPC	OO	GWR 175TH ANNIVERSARY
43176	**FB**	A	EFPC	OO	
43177	**FB**	A	EFPC	OO	
43179	**FB**	A	EFPC	OO	Pride of Laira
43180	**FB**	P	EFPC	OO	
43181	**FB**	A	EFPC	OO	
43182	**FB**	A	EFPC	OO	
43183	**FB**	A	EFPC	OO	
43185	**FB**	A	EFPC	OO	Great Western
43186	**FB**	A	EFPC	OO	
43187	**FB**	A	EFPC	OO	
43188	**FB**	A	EFPC	OO	

43189	**FB**	A	EFPC	OO	RAILWAY HERITAGE TRUST
43190	**FB**	A	EFPC	OO	
43191	**FB**	A	EFPC	OO	
43192	**FB**	A	EFPC	OO	
43193	**FB**	P	EFPC	OO	
43194	**FB**	FG	EFPC	OO	
43195	**FB**	P	EFPC	OO	
43196	**FB**	P	EFPC	OO	
43197	**FB**	P	EFPC	OO	
43198	**FB**	FG	EFPC	OO	Oxfordshire 2007

Class 43/2. Rebuilt East Coast, CrossCountry and Grand Central power cars. Power cars have been renumbered by adding 200 to their original number or 400 to their original number (Grand Central), except 43123 which became 43423.

43206 (43006)	**EC**	A	IECP	EC	
43207 (43007)	**XC**	A	EHPC	EC	
43208 (43008)	**NX**	A	IECP	EC	Lincolnshire Echo
43238 (43038)	**EC**	A	IECP	EC	
43239 (43039)	**EC**	A	IECP	EC	
43251 (43051)	**EC**	P	IECP	EC	
43257 (43057)	**EC**	P	IECP	EC	
43272 (43072)	**EC**	P	IECP	EC	
43274 (43074)	**EC**	P	IECP	EC	
43277 (43077)	**EC**	P	IECP	EC	
43285 (43085)	**XC**	P	EHPC	EC	
43290 (43090)	**EC**	P	IECP	EC	mtu fascination of power
43295 (43095)	**EC**	A	IECP	EC	
43296 (43096)	**EC**	A	IECP	EC	
43299 (43099)	**EC**	P	IECP	EC	
43300 (43100)	**EC**	P	IECP	EC	Craigentinny 100 YEARS 1914–2014
43301 (43101)	**XC**	P	EHPC	EC	
43302 (43102)	**EC**	P	IECP	EC	
43303 (43103)	**XC**	P	EHPC	EC	
43304 (43104)	**XC**	A	EHPC	EC	
43305 (43105)	**EC**	A	IECP	EC	
43306 (43106)	**EC**	A	IECP	EC	
43307 (43107)	**EC**	A	IECP	EC	
43308 (43108)	**EC**	A	IECP	EC	HIGHLAND CHIEFTAIN
43309 (43109)	**EC**	A	IECP	EC	
43310 (43110)	**EC**	A	IECP	EC	
43311 (43111)	**EC**	A	IECP	EC	
43312 (43112)	**EC**	A	IECP	EC	
43313 (43113)	**EC**	A	IECP	EC	
43314 (43114)	**EC**	A	IECP	EC	
43315 (43115)	**EC**	A	IECP	EC	
43316 (43116)	**EC**	A	IECP	EC	
43317 (43117)	**EC**	A	IECP	EC	
43318 (43118)	**EC**	A	IECP	EC	
43319 (43119)	**EC**	A	IECP	EC	

43320	(43120)	**NX**	A	IECP	EC	
43321	(43121)	**XC**	P	EHPC	EC	
43357	(43157)	**XC**	P	EHPC	EC	
43366	(43166)	**XC**	A	EHPC	EC	
43367	(43167)	**EC**	A	IECP	EC	DELTIC 50 1955–2005
43378	(43178)	**XC**	A	EHPC	EC	
43384	(43184)	**XC**	A	EHPC	EC	
43423	(43123) †	**GC**	A	GCHP	HT	'VALENTA' 1972–2010
43465	(43065) †	**GC**	A	GCHP	HT	
43467	(43067) †	**GC**	A	GCHP	HT	
43468	(43068) †	**GC**	A	GCHP	HT	
43480	(43080) †	**GC**	A	GCHP	HT	
43484	(43084) †	**GC**	A	GCHP	HT	PETER FOX 1942–2011
						PLATFORM 5

CLASS 47   BR/BRUSH/SULZER   Co-Co

Built: 1963–67 by Brush Traction, at Loughborough or by BR at Crewe Works.
Engine: Sulzer 12LDA28C of 1920 kW (2580 hp) at 750 rpm.
Main Generator: Brush TG160-60 Mk4 or TM172-50 Mk1.
Traction Motors: Brush TM64-68 Mk1 or Mk1A.
Maximum Tractive Effort: 267 kN (60000 lbf).
Continuous Tractive Effort: 133 kN (30000 lbf) at 26 mph.
Power at Rail: 1550 kW (2080 hp).   **Train Brakes:** Air.
Brake Force: 61 t.   **Dimensions:** 19.38 x 2.79 m.
Weight: 111.5–120.6 t.   **Wheel Diameter:** 1143 mm.
Design Speed: 95 mph.
Maximum Speed: 95 mph (* 75 mph).
Fuel Capacity: 3273 (+ 5887).   **RA:** 6 or 7.
Train Supply: Not equipped.
Multiple Working: m Green Circle (operational locos only).

Originally numbered in series D1100–D1111, D1500–D1999 but not in order.

Non-standard liveries/numbering:

47270   Also carries the number 1971.
47773   Also carries the number D1755.
47812   Also carries the number D1916.

Class 47/0 (Dual-braked locos) or Class 47/2 (Air-braked locos). Standard Design. Details as above.

47194	a+	**F**	WC	AWCX	CS (S)	
47236	+	**FE**	WC	AWCX	CS (S)	
47237	x+	**WC**	WC	AWCA	CS	
47245	x+m	**WC**	WC	AWCA	CS	
47270	a+	**B**	WC	AWCA	CS	SWIFT

Class 47/3 (Dual-braked locos) or Class 47/2 (Air-braked locos).
Details as Class 47/0 except: **Weight:** 113.7 t.

47355	am+	**K**	WC	AWCX	CS (S)
47368	x	**F**	WC	AWCX	CS (S)

Class 47/4. Electric Train Supply equipment.
Details as Class 47/0 except:

Weight: 120.4–125.1 t.	**Fuel Capacity:** 3273 (+ 5537) litres.
Train Supply: Electric. ETH 66.	**RA:** 7.

47492	x	**RX**	WC	AWCX	CS (S)
47500	x	**WC**	WC	AWCX	CS (S)
47501	xm+	**DS**	DR	XHSS	NC (S)	Craftsman
47526	x	**BL**	WC	AWCX	CS (S)
47580	x	**BL**	47	MBDL	TM	County of Essex

Class 47/7. Former Railnet dedicated locos. All have twin fuel tanks.

47727	m	**CS**	CS	COLO	WH	Rebecca
47739	m	**CS**	CS	COLO	WH	Robin of Templecombe 1938–2013
47746	x	**WC**	WC	AWCA	CS	
47749	m	**CS**	CS	COLO	WH	Demelza
47760	x	**WC**	WC	AWCA	CS	
47768		**RX**	WC	AWCX	CS (S)	
47769		**V**	HN	HNRS	BH (S)	Resolve
47772	x	**RX**	WC	AWCX	CS (S)	
47773	x	**GG**	70	MBDL	TM	
47776	x	**RX**	WC	AWCX	CS (S)	
47786		**WC**	WC	AWCA	CS	Roy Castle OBE
47787		**WC**	WC	AWCX	CS (S)	Windsor Castle
47790	m	**VN**	DR	XHNB	KM	Galloway Princess

Class 47/4 continued. RA6. Most fitted with extended-range fuel tanks (+).

47798	x	**RP**	NM	MBDL	YK	Prince William
47802	+m	**DS**	WC	AWCA	CS	
47804		**WC**	WC	AWCA	CS	
47805	+m	**DS**	DR	XHAC	KM	John Scott 12.5.45–22.5.12
47810	+m	**DI**	DR	XHAC	KM	Peter Bath MBE 1927–2006
47811		**GL**	FL	DHLT	BA (S)	
47812	+m	**GG**	RV	GBDF	BH	
47813	+m	**DS**	DR	XHNB	KM	Solent
47815	+m	**RB**	RV	GBDF	BH	GREAT WESTERN
47816	+	**GL**	FL	DFLH	BA (S)	
47818	+m	**DS**	DR	XHAC	KM	
47826		**WC**	WC	AWCA	CS	
47828	+m	**DS**	DR	XHAC	KM	
47830	+	**GL**	FL	DFLH	BH (S)	
47832	+m	**WC**	WC	AWCA	CS	
47841	+m	**DS**	DR	XHAC	KM	
47843	+m	**RB**	RV	GBDF	BH	VULCAN
47847	+m	**BL**	RV	RTLO	CD	
47848	+m	**RB**	RV	GBDF	BH	TITAN STAR
47851	+	**WC**	WC	AWCA	CS	
47853	+m	**DS**	DR	XHAC	KM	RAIL EXPRESS
47854	+	**WC**	WC	AWCA	CS	Diamond Jubilee

CLASS 50   ENGLISH ELECTRIC   Co-Co

Built: 1967–68 by English Electric at Vulcan Foundry, Newton-le-Willows.
Engine: English Electric 16CVST of 2010 kW (2700 hp) at 850 rpm.
Main Generator: English Electric 840/4B.
Traction Motors: English Electric 538/5A.
Maximum Tractive Effort: 216 kN (48500 lbf).
Continuous Tractive Effort: 147 kN (33000 lbf) at 23.5 mph.
Power at Rail: 1540 kW (2070 hp).   **Train Brakes:** Air & vacuum.
Brake Force: 59 t.   **Dimensions:** 20.88 x 2.78 m.
Weight: 116.9 t.   **Wheel Diameter:** 1092 mm.
Design Speed: 105 mph.   **Maximum Speed:** 90 mph.
Fuel Capacity: 4796 litres.   **RA:** 6.
Train Supply: Electric, index 61. **Multiple Working:** Orange Square.

Originally numbered D407, D444 & D449.

50007	B	NB	MBDL	WH	Hercules
50044	B	50	CFOL	KR	Exeter
50049	BL	50	CFOL	KR	Defiance

CLASS 52   BR/MAYBACH   C-C

Built: 1961–64 by BR at Swindon Works.
Engine: Two Maybach MD655 of 1007 kW (1350 hp) at 1500 rpm.
Transmission: Hydraulic. Voith L630rV.
Maximum Tractive Effort: 297 kN (66700 lbf).
Continuous Tractive Effort: 201 kN (45200 lbf) at 14.5 mph.
Power at Rail: 1490 kW (2000 hp).   **Train Brakes:** Air & vacuum.
Brake Force: 83 t.   **Dimensions:** 20.7 m x 2.78 m.
Weight: 110 t.   **Wheel Diameter:** 1092 mm.
Design Speed: 90 mph.   **Maximum Speed:** 90 mph.
Fuel Capacity: 3900 litres.   **RA:** 6.
Train Supply: Steam.   **Multiple Working:** Not equipped.

Never allocated a number in the 1972 number series.

Registered on TOPS as No. 89416.

| D1015 | M | DT | MBDL | TM | WESTERN CHAMPION |

CLASS 55   ENGLISH ELECTRIC   Co-Co

Built: 1961 by English Electric at Vulcan Foundry, Newton-le-Willows.
Engine: Two Napier-Deltic D18-25 of 1230 kW (1650 hp) each at 1500 rpm.
Main Generators: Two English Electric 829/1A.
Traction Motors: English Electric 538/A.
Maximum Tractive Effort: 222 kN (50000 lbf).
Continuous Tractive Effort: 136 kN (30500 lbf) at 32.5 mph.
Power at Rail: 1969 kW (2640 hp).   **Train Brakes:** Air & vacuum.
Brake Force: 51 t.   **Dimensions:** 21.18 x 2.68 m.
Weight: 100 t.   **Wheel Diameter:** 1092 mm.

Design Speed: 105 mph.   **Maximum Speed:** 100 mph.
Fuel Capacity: 3755 litres.   **RA:** 5.
Train Supply: Electric, index 66.   **Multiple Working:** Not equipped.

Originally numbered D9002, D9009 & D9000.

55022 registered on TOPS as No. 89500.

55002	B	NM	MBDL	YK	THE KING'S OWN YORKSHIRE LIGHT INFANTRY
55009	GG	DP	MBDL	BH	ALYCIDON
55022	B	MW	MBDL	Bo'ness	ROYAL SCOTS GREY

CLASS 56   BRUSH/BR/RUSTON   Co-Co

Built: 1976–84 by Electroputere at Craiova, Romania (as sub contractors for Brush) or BREL at Doncaster or Crewe Works.
Engine: Ruston Paxman 16RK3CT of 2460 kW (3250 hp) at 900 rpm.
Main Alternator: Brush BA1101A.
Traction Motors: Brush TM73-62.
Maximum Tractive Effort: 275 kN (61800 lbf).
Continuous Tractive Effort: 240 kN (53950 lbf) at 16.8 mph.
Power at Rail: 1790 kW (2400 hp).   **Train Brakes:** Air.
Brake Force: 60 t.   **Dimensions:** 19.36 x 2.79 m.
Weight: 126 t.   **Wheel Diameter:** 1143 mm.
Design Speed: 80 mph.   **Maximum Speed:** 80 mph.
Fuel Capacity: 5228 litres.   **RA:** 7.
Train Supply: Not equipped.   **Multiple Working:** Red Diamond.

All equipped with Slow Speed Control.

Class 56s exported for use abroad are listed in section 6 of this book.

Non-standard liveries: 56009 All over blue.

56081, 56098 and 56104 Unbranded Railfreight grey.

56303 All over dark green.

56311 Light grey with yellow cabsides.

56007	B	UR	MBDL	LR (S)
56009	O	UR	MBDL	BL (S)
56018	FER	UR	MBDL	LB (S)
56031	FER	UR	MBDL	LR (S)
56032	FER	UR	MBDL	WH (S)
56037	E	UR	MBDL	BL (S)
56038	FER	UR	MBDL	LR (S)
56049	FER	CS	COLS	WH (S)
56051	FER	CS	COLS	WH (S)
56060	FER	UR	MBDL	WH (S)
56065	FER	UR	MBDL	LR (S)
56069	FER	UR	MBDL	LR (S)
56077	LH	UR	MBDL	BL (S)
56078	CS	CS	COFS	WH

56081	**0**	UR	MBDL	LR (S)
56087	**CS**	CS	COFS	WH
56090	**FER**	CS	COLS	WH (S)
56091	**FER**	BA	HTLX	WH
56094	**CS**	CS	COFS	WH
56096	**CS**	CS	COFS	WH
56098	**0**	UR	MBDL	LR (S)
56103	**FER**	BA	HTLX	WH
56104	**0**	UR	MBDL	LR (S)
56105	**CS**	CS	COFS	WH
56106	**FER**	UR	MBDL	LR (S)
56113	**CS**	CS	COFS	WH
56128	**F**	BA	HTLX	WH (S)

56301	(56045)	**FA**	56	HTLX	WH
56302	(56124)	**CS**	CS	COFS	WH
56303	(56125)	**0**	BA	HTLX	WH
56311	(56057)	**0**	BA	HTLX	WH
56312	(56003)	**DC**	BA	HTLX	WH

56312: Jeremiah Dixon Son of County Durham Surveyor of the Mason-Dixon Line U.S.A.

CLASS 57   BRUSH/GM   Co-Co

Built: 1964–65 by Brush Traction at Loughborough or BR at Crewe Works as Class 47. Rebuilt 1997–2004 by Brush Traction at Loughborough.
Engine: General Motors 12 645 E3 of 1860 kW (2500 hp) at 904 rpm.
Main Alternator: Brush BA1101D (recovered from Class 56).
Traction Motors: Brush TM64-68 Mark 1 or Mark 1a.
Maximum Tractive Effort: 244.5 kN (55000 lbf).
Continuous Tractive Effort: 140 kN (31500 lbf) at ?? mph.
Power at Rail: 1507 kW (2025 hp).   **Train Brakes:** Air.
Brake Force: 80 t.   **Dimensions:** 19.38 x 2.79 m.
Weight: 120.6 t.   **Wheel Diameter:** 1143 mm.
Design Speed: 75 mph.   **Maximum Speed:** 75 mph.
Fuel Capacity: 5550 litres.   **RA:** 6
Train Supply: Not equipped.   **Multiple Working:** † DRS system.

Class 57/0. No Train Supply Equipment. Rebuilt 1997–2000.

57001	(47356)		**WC**	WC	AWCA	CS
57002	(47322)	†	**DS**	P	XHCK	KM
57003	(47317)	†	**DS**	P	XHSS	ZG (S)
57004	(47347)	†	**DS**	DR	XHCK	KM
57005	(47350)		**AZ**	WC	AWCX	CS (S)
57006	(47187)		**WC**	WC	AWCA	CS
57007	(47332)	†	**DS**	P	XHCK	KM
57008	(47060)	†	**DS**	P	XHCK	KM
57009	(47079)	†	**DS**	P	XHCK	KM
57010	(47231)	†	**DS**	P	XHCK	KM
57011	(47329)	†	**DS**	P	XHCK	KM
57012	(47204)	†	**DS**	P	XHCK	KM

Class 57/3. Electric Train Supply Equipment. Former Virgin Trains locos. Rebuilt 2002–04. Details as Class 57/0 except:

Engine: General Motors 12645F3B of 2050 kW (2750 hp) at 954 rpm.
Main Alternator: Brush BA1101F (recovered from a Class 56) or Brush BA1101G.
Fuel Capacity: 5887 litres. **Train Supply:** Electric, index 100.
Design Speed: 95 mph. **Maximum Speed:** 95 mph.
Brake Force: 60 t. **Weight:** 117 t.

57301	(47845)	i	**DI** DR XHAC	KM	Goliath
57302	(47827)	d	**DS** P XHVT	KM	Chad Varah
57303	(47705)	d	**DI** DR XHAC	KM	Pride of Carlisle
57304	(47807)	d	**DS** P XHVT	KM	Pride of Cheshire
57305	(47822)	d	**VN** DR XHAC	KM	Northern Princess
57306	(47814)	i	**Y** DR XHAC	KM	
57307	(47225)	d	**DR** P XHVT	KM	LADY PENELOPE
57308	(47846)	d	**DS** P XHVT	KM	County of Staffordshire
57309	(47806)	d	**DS** P XHVT	KM	Pride of Crewe
57310	(47831)	d	**DI** DR XHAC	KM	Pride of Cumbria
57311	(47817)	d	**DS** P XHVT	KM	Thunderbird
57312	(47330)	d	**VN** DR XHAC	KM	Solway Princess
57313	(47371)		**WC** WC AWCA	CS	
57314	(47372)		**WC** WC AWCA	CS	
57315	(47234)		**WC** WC AWCA	CS	
57316	(47290)		**AB** WC AWCA	CS	

Class 57/6. Electric Train Supply Equipment. Prototype ETS loco. Rebuilt 2001. Details as Class 57/0 except:

Main Alternator: Brush BA1101E. **Fuel Capacity:** 3273 litres.
Train Supply: Electric, index 95. **Weight:** 113 t.
Design Speed: 95 mph. **Maximum Speed:** 95 mph.
Brake Force: 60 t.

57601	(47825)	**WC** WC AWCA	CS	

Class 57/6. Electric Train Supply Equipment. First Great Western locos. Rebuilt 2004. Details as Class 57/3.

57602	(47337)	**FB** P EFOO	OO	Restormel Castle
57603	(47349)	**FB** P EFOO	OO	Tintagel Castle
57604	(47209)	**GW** P EFOO	OO	PENDENNIS CASTLE
57605	(47206)	**FB** P EFOO	OO	Totnes Castle

CLASS 58 BREL/RUSTON Co-Co

Built: 1983–87 by BREL at Doncaster Works.
Engine: Ruston Paxman 12RK3ACT of 2460 kW (3300 hp) at 1000 rpm.
Main Alternator: Brush BA1101B. **Traction Motors:** Brush TM73-62.
Maximum Tractive Effort: 275 kN (61800 lbf).
Continuous Tractive Effort: 240 kN (53950 lbf) at 17.4 mph.
Power at Rail: 1780 kW (2387 hp). **Train Brakes:** Air.
Brake Force: 60 t. **Dimensions:** 19.13 x 2.72 m.
Weight: 130 t. **Wheel Diameter:** 1120 mm.

Design Speed: 80 mph.   **Maximum Speed:** 80 mph.
Fuel Capacity: 4214 litres.   **RA:** 7.
Train Supply: Not equipped.   **Multiple Working:** Red Diamond.

All equipped with Slow Speed Control.

Class 58s exported for use abroad are listed in section 6 of this book.

58008	**ML**	DB	WQDA	EH (S)
58012	**F**	DB	WQCA	TO (S)
58022	**F**	DB	WQCA	CE (S)
58023	**ML**	DB	WQCA	TO (S)
58048	**E**	DB	WQCA	CE (S)

CLASS 59   GENERAL MOTORS   Co-Co

Built: 1985 (59001–004) or 1989 (59005) by General Motors, La Grange, Illinois, USA or 1990 (59101–104), 1994 (59201) and 1995 (59202–206) by General Motors, London, Ontario, Canada.
Engine: General Motors 16-645E3C two stroke of 2460 kW (3300 hp) at 904 rpm.
Main Alternator: General Motors AR11 MLD-D14A.
Traction Motors: General Motors D77B.
Maximum Tractive Effort: 506 kN (113 550 lbf).
Continuous Tractive Effort: 291 kN (65 300 lbf) at 14.3 mph.
Power at Rail: 1889 kW (2533 hp).   **Train Brakes:** Air.
Brake Force: 69 t.   **Dimensions:** 21.35 x 2.65 m.
Weight: 121 t.   **Wheel Diameter:** 1067 mm.
Design Speed: 60 (* 75) mph.   **Maximum Speed:** 60 (* 75) mph.
Fuel Capacity: 4546 litres.   **RA:** 7.
Train Supply: Not equipped.   **Multiple Working:** AAR System.

59003 was due to be repatriated from Germany as this book closed for press, having been purchased by GB Railfreight.

Non-standard livery: 59003 Heavy Haul Power International (red & dark blue).

Class 59/0. Owned by Aggregate Industries and GB Railfreight.

59001	**AI**	AI	XYPO	MD	YEOMAN ENDEAVOUR
59002	**AI**	AI	XYPO	MD	ALAN J DAY
59003	**0**	GB	GBYH	PG	YEOMAN HIGHLANDER
59004	**FY**	AI	XYPO	MD	PAUL A HAMMOND
59005	**AI**	AI	XYPO	MD	KENNETH J PAINTER

Class 59/1. Owned by Hanson Quarry Products.

59101	**HA**	HA	XYPA	MD	Village of Whatley
59102	**HA**	HA	XYPA	MD	Village of Chantry
59103	**HA**	HA	XYPA	MD	Village of Mells
59104	**HA**	HA	XYPA	MD	Village of Great Elm

Class 59/2. Owned by DB Schenker.

| 59201 | * | **DB** | DB | WDAM | MD |

59202	*	**DB**	DB	WDAM	MD	Alan Meddows Taylor
						MD Mendip Rail Limited
59203	*	**DB**	DB	WDAM	MD	
59204	*	**DB**	DB	WDAM	MD	
59205	*b	**DB**	DB	WDAM	MD	
59206	*b	**DB**	DB	WDAM	MD	John F. Yeoman Rail Pioneer

CLASS 60   BRUSH/MIRRLEES   Co-Co

Built: 1989–93 by Brush Traction at Loughborough.
Engine: Mirrlees 8MB275T of 2310 kW (3100 hp) at 1000 rpm.
Main Alternator: Brush BA1006A.
Traction Motors: Brush TM2161A.
Maximum Tractive Effort: 500 kN (106500 lbf).
Continuous Tractive Effort: 336 kN (71570 lbf) at 17.4 mph.
Power at Rail: 1800 kW (2415 hp).   **Train Brakes:** Air.
Brake Force: 74 (+ 62) t.   **Dimensions:** 21.34 x 2.64 m.
Weight: 129 (+ 131) t.   **Wheel Diameter:** 1118 mm.
Design Speed: 62 mph.   **Maximum Speed:** 60 mph.
Fuel Capacity: 4546 (+ 5225) litres.   **RA:** 8.
Train Supply: Not equipped.   **Multiple Working:** Within class.

All equipped with Slow Speed Control.

* Refurbished locos.

60034, 60064, 60072, 60073, 60077, 60084 and 60090 carry their names on one side only.

60500 originally carried the number 60016.

Advertising liveries: 60066 Powering Drax (silver).

60099 Tata Steel (silver).

60001	*	**DB**	DB	WCAT	TO	
60002	+	E	CS	COLS	TO (S)	
60003	+	E	DB	WQBA	TO (S)	FREIGHT TRANSPORT ASSOCIATION
60004	+	E	DB	WQBA	TO (S)	
60005	+	E	DB	WQBA	TO (S)	
60006		CU	DB	WQBA	TO (S)	
60007	+*	**DB**	DB	WQAA	TO (S)	The Spirit of Tom Kendell
60008		E	DB	WQBA	TO (S)	Sir William McAlpine
60009	+	E	DB	WQBA	TO (S)	
60010	+*	**DB**	DB	WCBT	TO	
60011		**DB**	DB	WCAT	TO	
60012	+	E	DB	WQBA	TO (S)	
60013		EG	DB	WQDA	TO (S)	Robert Boyle
60014		EG	DB	WQBA	TO (S)	
60015	+*	**DB**	DB	WCBT	TO	
60017	+*	**DB**	DB	WCBT	TO	
60018		E	DB	WQBA	TO (S)	
60019	*	**DB**	DB	WCAT	TO	Port of Grimsby & Immingham
60020	+*	**DB**	DB	WCBT	TO	

60021 +	CS	CS	COLO	RU	
60022 +	E	DB	WQBA	TO (S)	
60023 +	E	DB	WQBA	TO (S)	
60024 *	DB	DB	WCAT	TO	Clitheroe Castle
60025 +	E	DB	WQBA	TO (S)	
60026 +	E	CS	COLS	TO (S)	
60027 +	E	DB	WQBA	TO (S)	
60028 +	EG	DB	WQDA	CE (S)	
60029	E	DB	WQDA	CE (S)	
60030 +	E	DB	WQBA	TO (S)	
60031	E	DB	WQBA	TO (S)	
60032	F	DB	WQBA	TO (S)	
60033 +	CU	DB	WQDA	TO (S)	Tees Steel Express
60034	EG	DB	WQBA	TO (S)	Carnedd Llewelyn
60035	E	DB	WCAT	TO	
60036	E	DB	WQBA	TO (S)	GEFCO
60037 +	E	DB	WQBA	TO (S)	
60038 +	E	DB	WQDA	CE (S)	
60039 *	DB	DB	WCAT	TO	
60040 *	DB	DB	WCAT	TO	The Territorial Army Centenary
60041 +	E	DB	WQDA	TO (S)	
60042	E	DB	WQBA	TO (S)	
60043	E	DB	WQBA	TO (S)	
60044 *	DB	DB	WCAT	TO	
60045	E	DB	WCAT	TO	The Permanent Way Institution
60046 +	EG	DB	WQDA	CE (S)	
60047	E	CS	COLS	TO (S)	
60048	E	DB	WQDA	TO (S)	
60049	E	DB	WCAT	TO	
60050	E	DB	WQBA	TO (S)	
60051 +	E	DB	WQBA	TO (S)	
60052 +	E	DB	WQBA	TO (S)	Glofa Twr – The last deep mine in Wales – Tower Colliery
60053	E	DB	WQBA	TO (S)	
60054 +*	DB	DB	WCBT	TO	
60055 +	EG	DB	WQDA	CE (S)	
60056 +	EG	CS	COLS	TO (S)	
60057	EG	DB	WQBA	TO (S)	Adam Smith
60058 +	E	DB	WQBA	TO (S)	
60059 +*	DB	DB	WCBT	TO	Swinden Dalesman
60060	EG	DB	WQBA	TO (S)	
60061	F	DB	WQDA	TO (S)	
60062 *	DB	DB	WCAT	TO	Stainless Pioneer
60063 *	DB	DB	WCAT	TO	
60064 +	EG	DB	WQBA	TO (S)	Back Tor
60065	E	DB	WCAT	TO	Spirit of JAGUAR
60066 *	AL	DB	WQAA	TO (S)	
60067	EG	DB	WQBA	TO (S)	
60068	EG	DB	WQBA	TO (S)	
60069	E	DB	WQBA	TO (S)	Slioch
60070 +	F	DB	WQBA	TO (S)	John Loudon McAdam

60071	+	E	DB	WCBT	TO	Ribblehead Viaduct
60072		EG	DB	WQBA	TO (S)	Cairn Toul
60073		EG	DB	WQBA	TO (S)	Cairn Gorm
60074	*	DB	DB	WCAT	TO
60075		E	DB	WQBA	TO (S)
60076		EG	CS	COLS	TO (S)
60077	+	EG	DB	WQBA	TO (S)	Canisp
60078		ML	DB	WQBA	TO (S)
60079	*	DB	DB	WCAT	TO
60080	+	E	DB	WQBA	TO (S)
60081	+	GW	DB	WQBA	TO (S)
60082		EG	DB	WQBA	CE (S)
60083		E	DB	WQBA	TO (S)
60084		EG	DB	WQBA	TO (S)	Cross Fell
60085		E	CS	COLS	TO (S)
60086		EG	DB	WQBA	TO (S)
60087		CS	CS	COLO	RU	CLIC Sargent www.clicsargent.co.uk
60088		F	DB	WQBA	TO (S)
60089	+	E	DB	WQBA	TO (S)
60090	+	EG	DB	WQBA	TO (S)	Quinag
60091	+*	DB	DB	WCBT	TO	Barry Needham
60092	+*	DB	DB	WCBT	TO
60093		E	DB	WQBA	TO (S)
60094		E	DB	WQBA	TO (S)	Rugby Flyer
60095		EG	CS	COLS	TO (S)
60096		E	CS	COLS	TO (S)
60097	+	E	DB	WQBA	TO (S)
60098	+	E	DB	WQBA	TO (S)
60099		AL	DB	WCAT	TO
60100	*	DB	DB	WCAT	TO
60500		E	DB	WQBA	TO (S)

CLASS 66   GENERAL MOTORS/EMD   Co-Co

Built: 1998–2008 by General Motors/EMD, London, Ontario, Canada (Model JT42CWR (low emission locos Model JT42CWRM)) or 2013–14 by EMD/Progress Rail, Muncie, Indiana (66752–772).
Engine: General Motors 12N-710G3B-EC two stroke of 2385 kW (3200 hp) at 904 rpm (low emission locos General Motors 12N-710G3B-T2).
Main Alternator: General Motors AR8/CA6.
Traction Motors: General Motors D43TR.
Maximum Tractive Effort: 409 kN (92000 lbf).
Continuous Tractive Effort: 260 kN (58390 lbf) at 15.9 mph.
Power at Rail: 1850 kW (2480 hp).   **Train Brakes:** Air.
Brake Force: 68 t.   **Dimensions:** 21.35 x 2.64 m.
Weight: 127 t.   **Wheel Diameter:** 1120 mm.
Design Speed: 87.5 mph.   **Maximum Speed:** 75 mph (unless stated).
Fuel Capacity: 6550 litres (unless stated).   **RA:** 7.
Train Supply: Not equipped.   **Multiple Working:** AAR System.

All equipped with Slow Speed Control.

Class 66s previously used in the UK but now in use abroad are listed in section 6 of this book. Some of the 60 DBS 66s moved to France return to Great Britain from time to time for maintenance or operational requirements.

Advertising livery: 66048 Stobart Rail (two tone blue & white).

Class 66 delivery dates. The Class 66 design has evolved over a 16-year period, with over 400 locomotives delivered. For clarity the delivery dates (by year) for each batch of locos is as follows:

66001–250	EWS (now DB Schenker). 1998–2000 (some now in use in France or Poland).
66301–305	Fastline. 2008. Now used by DRS.
66401–410	DRS. 2003. Now in use with GB Railfreight or Colas Rail and renumbered 66733–737 and 66742–746 (66734 since scrapped).
66411–420	DRS. 2006. Now leased by Freightliner (66411/412/417 exported to Poland).
66421–430	DRS. 2007
66431–434	DRS. 2008
66501–505	Freightliner. 1999
66506–520	Freightliner. 2000
66521–525	Freightliner. 2000 (66521 since scrapped).
66526–531	Freightliner. 2001
66532–537	Freightliner. 2001
66538–543	Freightliner. 2001
66544–553	Freightliner. 2001
66554	Freightliner. 2002†
66555–566	Freightliner. 2002
66567–574	Freightliner. 2003. 66573–574 now used by Colas Rail and renumbered 66846–847.
66575–577	Freightliner. 2004. Now used by Colas Rail and renumbered 66848–850.
66578–581	Freightliner. 2005. Now used by GBRf and renumbered 66738–741.
66582–594	Freightliner. 2007 (66582/583/584/586 exported to Poland).
66595–599	Freightliner. 2008
66601–606	Freightliner. 2000
66607–612	Freightliner. 2002 (66607/609/611/612 exported to Poland)
66613–618	Freightliner. 2003
66619–622	Freightliner. 2005
66623–625	Freightliner. 2007 (66624/625 exported to Poland).
66701–707	GB Railfreight. 2001
66708–712	GB Railfreight. 2002
66713–717	GB Railfreight. 2003
66718–722	GB Railfreight. 2006
66723–727	GB Railfreight. 2006
66728–732	GB Railfreight. 2008
66747–749	Built in 2008 as 20078968-004/006/007 (DE 6313/15/16) for Crossrail AG in the Netherlands but never used. Sold to GB Railfreight in 2012.
66750–751	Built in 2003 as 20038513-01/04 and have worked in the Netherlands, Germany and Poland. GBRf secured these two locomotives on lease in 2013.

66752–772 GB Railfreight. 2014.
66951–952 Freightliner. 2004
66953–957 Freightliner. 2008

† Replacement for 66521, written off in the Great Heck accident in 2001.

Class 66/0. DB Schenker-operated locos.

All fitted with Swinghead Automatic "Buckeye" Combination Couplers except 66001 and 66002.

† Fitted with additional lights and drawgear for Lickey banking duties.

t Fitted with tripcocks for working over London Underground tracks between Harrow-on-the-Hill and Amersham.

66001 t	**DB**	A	WBTT	TO	
66002	E	A	WBAT	TO	Lafarge Quorn
66003	E	A	WBAT	TO	
66004	E	A	WBAT	TO	
66005	E	A	WBAT	TO	
66006	E	A	WBAT	TO	
66007	E	A	WBAT	TO	
66008	E	A	WBAT	TO	
66009	E	A	WBAT	TO	
66011	E	A	WBAT	TO	
66012	E	A	WBAT	TO	
66013	E	A	WBAT	TO	
66014	E	A	WBAT	TO	
66015	E	A	WBAT	TO	
66016	E	A	WBAT	TO	
66017 t	E	A	WBTT	TO	
66018	E	A	WBAT	TO	
66019 t	E	A	WBTT	TO	
66020	E	A	WBAT	TO	
66021	E	A	WBAT	TO	
66023	E	A	WBAT	TO	
66024	E	A	WBAT	TO	
66025	E	A	WBAT	TO	
66027	E	A	WBAT	TO	
66030	E	A	WBAT	TO	
66031	E	A	WBAT	TO	
66034	E	A	WBAT	TO	
66035	E	A	WBAT	TO	
66037	E	A	WBAT	TO	
66039	E	A	WBAT	TO	
66040	E	A	WBAT	TO	
66041	E	A	WBAT	TO	
66043	E	A	WBAT	TO	
66044	E	A	WBAT	TO	
66046	E	A	WBAT	TO	
66047	E	A	WBAT	TO	
66048	**AL**	A	WQDA	TO (S)	James the Engine
66050	E	A	WBAT	TO	EWS Energy

66051	E	A	WBAT	TO	
66053	E	A	WBAT	TO	
66054	E	A	WBAT	TO	
66055 †	E	A	WBLT	TO	
66056 †	E	A	WBLT	TO	
66057 †	E	A	WBLT	TO	
66058 †	E	A	WBLT	TO	
66059 †	E	A	WBLT	TO	
66060	E	A	WBAT	TO	
66061	E	A	WBAT	TO	
66063	E	A	WBAT	TO	
66065	E	A	WBAT	TO	
66066	E	A	WBAT	TO	
66067	E	A	WBAT	TO	
66068	E	A	WBAT	TO	
66069	E	A	WBAT	TO	
66070	E	A	WBAT	TO	
66074	E	A	WBAT	TO	
66075	E	A	WBAT	TO	
66076	E	A	WBAT	TO	
66077	E	A	WBAT	TO	Benjamin Gimbert G.C.
66078	E	A	WBAT	TO	
66079	E	A	WBAT	TO	James Nightall G.C.
66080	E	A	WBAT	TO	
66081	E	A	WBAT	TO	
66082	E	A	WBAT	TO	
66083	E	A	WBAT	TO	
66084	E	A	WBAT	TO	
66085	E	A	WBAT	TO	
66086	E	A	WBAT	TO	
66087	E	A	WBAT	TO	
66088	E	A	WBAT	TO	
66089	E	A	WBAT	TO	
66090	E	A	WBAT	TO	
66091	E	A	WBAT	TO	
66092	E	A	WBAT	TO	
66093	E	A	WBAT	TO	
66094	E	A	WBAT	TO	
66095	E	A	WBAT	TO	
66096	E	A	WBAT	TO	
66097	DB	A	WBAT	TO	
66098	E	A	WBAT	TO	
66099 r	E	A	WBBT	TO	
66100 r	E	A	WBBT	TO	
66101 r	DB	A	WBBT	TO	
66102 r	E	A	WBBT	TO	
66103 r	E	A	WBBT	TO	
66104 r	E	A	WBBT	TO	
66105 r	E	A	WBBT	TO	
66106 r	E	A	WBBT	TO	
66107 r	E	A	WBBT	TO	

66108 r	**E**	A	WBBT	TO	
66109	**E**	A	WBBT	TO	
66110 r	**E**	A	WBBT	TO	
66111 r	**E**	A	WBBT	TO	
66112 r	**E**	A	WBBT	TO	
66113 r	**E**	A	WBBT	TO	
66114 r	**DB**	A	WBBT	TO	
66115	**E**	A	WBAT	TO	
66116	**E**	A	WBAT	TO	
66117	**E**	A	WBAT	TO	
66118	**DB**	A	WBAT	TO	
66119	**E**	A	WBAT	TO	
66120	**E**	A	WBAT	TO	
66121	**E**	A	WBAT	TO	
66122	**E**	A	WBAT	TO	
66124	**E**	A	WBAT	TO	
66125	**E**	A	WBAT	TO	
66126	**E**	A	WBAT	TO	
66127	**E**	A	WBAT	TO	
66128	**E**	A	WBAT	TO	
66129	**E**	A	WBAT	TO	
66130	**E**	A	WBAT	TO	
66131	**E**	A	WBAT	TO	
66132	**E**	A	WBAT	TO	
66133	**E**	A	WBAT	TO	
66134	**E**	A	WBAT	TO	
66135	**E**	A	WBAT	TO	
66136	**E**	A	WBAT	TO	
66137	**E**	A	WBAT	TO	
66138	**E**	A	WBAT	TO	
66139	**E**	A	WBAT	TO	
66140	**E**	A	WBAT	TO	
66141	**E**	A	WQAA	TO (S)	
66142	**E**	A	WBAT	TO	
66143	**E**	A	WBAT	TO	
66144	**E**	A	WBAT	TO	
66145	**E**	A	WBAT	TO	
66147	**E**	A	WBAT	TO	
66148	**E**	A	WBAT	TO	
66149	**E**	A	WBAT	TO	
66150	**E**	A	WBAT	TO	
66151	**E**	A	WBAT	TO	
66152	**DB**	A	WBAT	TO	Derek Holmes Railway Operator
66154	**E**	A	WBAT	TO	
66155	**E**	A	WBAT	TO	
66156	**E**	A	WBAT	TO	
66158	**E**	A	WBAT	TO	
66160	**E**	A	WBAT	TO	
66161	**E**	A	WBAT	TO	
66162	**E**	A	WBAT	TO	
66164	**E**	A	WBAT	TO	

66165	E	A	WBAT	TO	
66167	E	A	WBAT	TO	
66168	E	A	WBAT	TO	
66169	E	A	WBAT	TO	
66170	E	A	WBAT	TO	
66171	E	A	WBAT	TO	
66172	E	A	WBAT	TO	PAUL MELLENEY
66174	E	A	WBAT	TO	
66175	E	A	WBAT	TO	
66176	E	A	WBAT	TO	
66177	E	A	WBAT	TO	
66181	E	A	WBAT	TO	
66182	E	A	WBAT	TO	
66183	E	A	WBAT	TO	
66184	E	A	WQAA	LT (S)	
66185	DB	A	WBAT	TO	DP WORLD London Gateway
66186	E	A	WBAT	TO	
66187	E	A	WBAT	TO	
66188	E	A	WBAT	TO	
66192	E	A	WBAT	TO	
66193	E	A	WBAT	TO	
66194	E	A	WBAT	TO	
66197	E	A	WBAT	TO	
66198	E	A	WBAT	TO	
66199	E	A	WBAT	TO	
66200	E	A	WBAT	TO	RAILWAY HERITAGE COMMITTEE
66201	E	A	WBAT	TO	
66204	E	A	WBAT	TO	
66206	E	A	WBAT	TO	
66207	E	A	WBAT	TO	
66213	E	A	WBAT	TO	
66221	E	A	WBAT	TO	
66230	E	A	WBAT	TO	
66232	E	A	WBAT	TO	
66238	E	A	WBAT	TO	
66250	E	A	WBAT	TO	

Class 66/3. Former Fastline-operated loco now operated by DRS. Low emission. Details as Class 66/0 except:

Engine: EMD 12N-710G3B-U2 two stroke of 2420 kW (3245 hp) at 904 rpm.
Traction Motors: General Motors D43TRC.
Fuel Capacity: 5150 litres.

66301	DS	PC	XHIM	KM
66302	DS	PC	XHIM	KM
66303	DS	PC	XHIM	KM
66304	DS	PC	XHIM	KM
66305	DS	PC	XHIM	KM

66413–434. Low emission. Macquarie Group-owned. Details as Class 66/0 except:

Engine: EMD 12N-710G3B-U2 two stroke of 2420 kW (3245 hp) at 904 rpm.
Traction Motors: General Motors D43TRC.
Fuel Capacity: 5150 litres.

Non-standard livery: 66414 Two tone blue & white (formerly Stobart Rail).

66413	**DS**	MQ	DFHG	LD
66414	**O**	MQ	DFIN	LD
66415	**DS**	MQ	DFHG	LD
66416	**FH**	MQ	DFIN	LD
66418	**DS**	MQ	DFIN	LD
66419	**DS**	MQ	DFHG	LD
66420	**DS**	MQ	DFIN	LD
66421	**DS**	MQ	XHIM	KM
66422	**DS**	MQ	XHIM	KM
66423	**DS**	MQ	XHIM	KM
66424	**DS**	MQ	XHIM	KM
66425	**DS**	MQ	XHIM	KM
66426	**DS**	MQ	XHIM	KM
66427	**DS**	MQ	XHIM	KM
66428	**DS**	MQ	XHIM	KM
66429	**DS**	MQ	XHIM	KM
66430	**DS**	MQ	XHIM	KM
66431	**DS**	MQ	XHIM	KM
66432	**DS**	MQ	XHIM	KM
66433	**DS**	MQ	XHIM	KM
66434	**DR**	MQ	XHIM	KM

Class 66/5. Freightliner-operated locos. Details as Class 66/0.

Advertising livery: 66522 Shanks Waste (one half of loco Freightliner green and one half Shanks' Waste light green).

66501	**FL**	P	DFIM	LD	Japan 2001
66502	**FL**	P	DFIM	LD	Basford Hall Centenary 2001
66503	**FL**	P	DFIM	LD	The RAILWAY MAGAZINE
66504	**FH**	P	DFIM	LD	
66505	**FL**	P	DFIM	LD	
66506	**FL**	E	DFHH	LD	Crewe Regeneration
66507	**FL**	E	DFHH	LD	
66508	**FL**	E	DFHH	LD	
66509	**FL**	E	DFHH	LD	
66510	**FL**	E	DFHH	LD	
66511	**FL**	E	DFHH	LD	
66512	**FL**	E	DFHH	LD	
66513	**FL**	E	DFHH	LD	
66514	**FL**	E	DFHH	LD	
66515	**FL**	E	DFHH	LD	
66516	**FL**	E	DFIM	LD	
66517	**FL**	E	DFIM	LD	
66518	**FL**	E	DFHH	LD	

66519	FL	E	DFHH	LD	
66520	FL	E	DFHH	LD	
66522	AL	E	DFHH	LD	
66523	FL	E	DFHH	LD	
66524	FL	E	DFHH	LD	
66525	FL	E	DFHH	LD	
66526	FL	P	DFHH	LD	Driver Steve Dunn (George)
66527	FL	P	DFHH	LD	Don Raider
66528	FL	P	DFHH	LD	
66529	FL	P	DFHH	LD	
66530	FL	P	DFHH	LD	
66531	FL	P	DFHH	LD	
66532	FL	P	DFIM	LD	P&O Nedlloyd Atlas
66533	FL	P	DFIM	LD	Hanjin Express/Senator Express
66534	FL	P	DFIM	LD	OOCL Express
66535	FL	P	DFHH	LD	
66536	FL	P	DFHH	LD	
66537	FL	P	DFIM	LD	
66538	FL	E	DFIM	LD	
66539	FL	E	DFHH	LD	
66540	FL	E	DFIM	LD	Ruby
66541	FL	E	DFIM	LD	
66542	FL	E	DFIM	LD	
66543	FL	E	DFIM	LD	
66544	FL	P	DFHH	LD	
66545	FL	P	DFHH	LD	
66546	FL	P	DFHH	LD	
66547	FL	P	DFHH	LD	
66548	FL	P	DFHH	LD	
66549	FL	P	DFHH	LD	
66550	FL	P	DFHH	LD	
66551	FL	P	DFHH	LD	
66552	FL	P	DFHH	LD	Maltby Raider
66553	FL	P	DFHH	LD	
66554	FL	E	DFHH	LD	
66555	FL	E	DFHH	LD	
66556	FL	E	DFIM	LD	
66557	FL	E	DFHH	LD	
66558	FL	E	DFIM	LD	
66559	FL	E	DFHH	LD	
66560	FL	E	DFHH	LD	
66561	FL	E	DFHH	LD	
66562	FL	E	DFHH	LD	
66563	FL	E	DFHH	LD	
66564	FL	E	DFHH	LD	
66565	FL	E	DFHH	LD	
66566	FL	E	DFIM	LD	
66567	FL	E	DFIM	LD	
66568	FL	E	DFIM	LD	
66569	FL	E	DFIM	LD	
66570	FL	E	DFIM	LD	

| 66571 | FL | E | DFIM | LD |
| 66572 | FL | E | DFIM | LD |

Class 66/5. Freightliner-operated low emission locos. Details as Class 66/0 except:

Engine: EMD 12N-710G3B-U2 two stroke of 2420 kW (3245 hp) at 904 rpm.
Traction Motors: General Motors D43TRC.
Fuel Capacity: 5150 litres.

66585	FL	MQ	DFHG	LD	The Drax Flyer
66587	FL	MQ	DFIN	LD	
66588	FL	MQ	DFIN	LD	
66589	FL	MQ	DFIN	LD	
66590	FL	MQ	DFIN	LD	
66591	FL	MQ	DFIN	LD	
66592	FL	MQ	DFIN	LD	Johnson Stevens Agencies
66593	FL	MQ	DFIN	LD	3MG MERSEY MULTIMODAL GATEWAY
66594	FL	MQ	DFIN	LD	NYK Spirit of Kyoto
66595	FL	PC	DFHG	LD	
66596	FL	PC	DFHG	LD	
66597	FL	PC	DFHG	LD	Viridor
66598	FL	PC	DFHG	LD	
66599	FL	PC	DFHG	LD	

Class 66/6. Freightliner-operated locomotives with modified gear ratios.
Details as Class 66/0 except:

Maximum Tractive Effort: 467 kN (105080 lbf).
Continuous Tractive Effort: 296 kN (66630 lbf) at 14.0 mph.
Design Speed: 65 mph.   **Maximum Speed:** 65 mph.

66601	FL	P	DFHH	LD	The Hope Valley
66602	FL	P	DFHH	LD	
66603	FL	P	DFHH	LD	
66604	FL	P	DFHH	LD	
66605	FL	P	DFHH	LD	
66606	FL	P	DFHH	LD	
66607	FL	P	DFHH	LD	
66610	FL	P	DFHH	LD	
66613	FL	E	DFHH	LD	
66614	FL	E	DFHH	LD	
66615	FL	E	DFHH	LD	
66616	FL	E	DFHH	LD	
66617	FL	E	DFHH	LD	
66618	FL	E	DFHH	LD	Railways Illustrated Annual Photographic Awards Alan Barnes
66619	FL	E	DFHH	LD	Derek W. Johnson MBE
66620	FL	E	DFHH	LD	
66621	FL	E	DFHH	LD	
66622	FL	E	DFHH	LD	

Class 66/6. Freightliner-operated low emission loco with modified gear ratios.
Fuel Capacity: 5150 litres.

Advertising livery: 66623 Bardon Aggregates (blue).

66623	**AL**	MQ	DFHG	LD	Bill Bolsover

Class 66/7. GB Railfreight-operated locos. Details as Class 66/0.

Non-standard/Advertising liveries:

66705 **GB** livery but with the addition of "Union Jack" bodyside vinyls.

66709 MSC – blue with images of a container ship.

66718 London Underground 150, black).

66720 Day and night (various colours, different on each side).

66721 London Underground 150 (white with tube map images).

66750 Rush Rail all over blue.

66701	**GB**	E	GBCM	PG	
66702	**GB**	E	GBCM	PG	Blue Lightning
66703	**GB**	E	GBCM	PG	Doncaster PSB 1981–2002
66704	**GB**	E	GBCM	PG	Colchester Power Signalbox
66705	**GB**	E	GBCM	PG	Golden Jubilee
66706	**GB**	E	GBCM	PG	Nene Valley
66707	**GB**	E	GBCM	PG	Sir Sam Fay GREAT CENTRAL RAILWAY
66708	**GB**	E	GBCM	PG	Jayne
66709	**AL**	E	GBCM	PG	Sorrento
66710	**GB**	E	GBCM	PG	Phil Packer BRIT
66711	**GB**	E	GBCM	PG	
66712	**GB**	E	GBCM	PG	Peterborough Power Signalbox
66713	**GB**	E	GBCM	PG	Forest City
66714	**GB**	E	GBCM	PG	Cromer Lifeboat
66715	**GB**	E	GBCM	PG	VALOUR – IN MEMORY OF ALL RAILWAY EMPLOYEES WHO GAVE THEIR LIVES FOR THEIR COUNTRY
66716	**GB**	E	GBCM	PG	LOCOMOTIVE & CARRIAGE INSTITUTION CENTENARY 1911–2011
66717	**GB**	E	GBCM	PG	Good Old Boy

66718–746. Low emission. GB Railfreight locos. 66733–737 renumbered from former DRS locos 66401–405. 66738–741 renumbered from former Freightliner locos 66578–581. 66742–746 renumbered from former DRS/Colas Rail locos 66406–410/841–845.

All details as Class 66/0 except 66718–732/747–749 as below:

Engine: EMD 12N-710G3B-U2 two stroke of 2420 kW (3245 hp) at 904 rpm.
Traction Motors: General Motors D43TRC.
Fuel Capacity: 5546 litres (66718–722) or 5150 litres (66723–732/747–749).

66747–749 were originally built for Crossrail AG in the Netherlands.

66750/751 were originally built for mainland Europe in 2003.

66718	**AL**	E	GBCM		PG	Sir Peter Hendy CBE
66719	**GB**	E	GBCM		PG	METRO-LAND
66720	**O**	E	GBCM		PG	
66721	**AL**	E	GBCM		PG	Harry Beck
66722	**GB**	E	GBCM		PG	Sir Edward Watkin
66723	**FS**	E	GBSD		PG	Chinook
66724	**FS**	E	GBSD		PG	Drax Power Station
66725	**FS**	E	GBSD		PG	SUNDERLAND
66726	**FS**	E	GBSD		PG	SHEFFIELD WEDNESDAY
66727	**FS**	E	GBSD		PG	Andrew Scott CBE
66728	**GB**	P	GBCM		PG	Institution of Railway Operators
66729	**GB**	P	GBCM		PG	DERBY COUNTY
66730	**GB**	P	GBCM		PG	Whitemoor
66731	**GB**	P	GBCM		PG	interhub GB
66732	**GB**	P	GBCM		PG	GBRf The First Decade 1999–2009
						John Smith – MD

66733	(66401)	r	**GB**	P	GBFM	PG	Cambridge PSB
66735	(66403)	r	**GB**	P	GBFM	PG	
66736	(66404)	r	**GB**	P	GBFM	PG	WOLVERHAMPTON WANDERERS
66737	(66405)	r	**GB**	P	GBFM	PG	Lesia
66738	(66578)		**GB**	PC	GBCM	PG	HUDDERSFIELD TOWN
66739	(66579)		**GB**	PC	GBCM	PG	Bluebell Railway
66740	(66580)		**GB**	PC	GBCM	PG	Sarah
66741	(66581)		**GB**	PC	GBCM	PG	

66742	(66406, 66841)	**GB**	PC	GBRT	PG	ABP Port of Immingham
						Centenary 1912–2012
66743	(66407, 66842)	**GB**	PC	GBRT	PG	
66744	(66408, 66843)	**GB**	PC	GBRT	PG	Crossrail
66745	(66409, 66844)	**GB**	PC	GBRT	PG	Modern Railways
						The first 50 Years
66746	(66410, 66845)	**GB**	PC	GBRT	PG	

66747	(20078968-007)	**U**	GB	GBNL	PG	
66748	(20078968-004)	**U**	GB	GBNL	PG	
66749	(20078968-006)	**U**	GB	GBNL	PG	
66750	(20038513-01)	**O**	PC	GBDR	PG	
66751	(20038513-04)	**GB**	PC	GBDR	PG	

66752–772. Low emission. Currently being delivered to GBRf.

Engine: EMD 12N-710G3B-U2 two stroke of 2420 kW (3245 hp) at 904 rpm.
Traction Motors: General Motors D43TRC.
Fuel Capacity: 6800 litres.

66752	**GB**	GB	GBNB	PG	The Hoosier State
66753	**GB**	GB	GBNB	PG	
66754	**GB**	GB	GBNB	PG	
66755	**GB**	GB	GBNB	PG	
66756	**GB**	GB	GBNB	PG	
66757	**GB**	GB	GBNB	PG	
66758	**GB**	GB	GBNB	PG	
66759	**GB**	GB	GBNB	PG	

66760	**GB**	GB	GBNB	PG
66761	**GB**	GB	GBNB	PG
66762	**GB**	GB	GBNB	PG
66763	**GB**	GB	GBNB	PG
66764	**GB**	GB	GBNB	PG
66765	**GB**	GB	GBNB	PG
66766	**GB**	GB		
66767	**GB**	GB		
66768	**GB**	GB		
66769	**GB**	GB		
66770	**GB**	GB		
66771	**GB**	GB		
66772	**GB**	GB		

Class 66/8. Colas Rail locos. Renumbered from former Freightliner locos 66573–577. Details as Class 66/0.

66846 (66573)	**CS**	CS	COLO	RU	
66847 (66574)	**CS**	CS	COLO	RU	
66848 (66575)	**CS**	CS	COLO	RU	
66849 (66576)	**CS**	CS	COLO	RU	Wylam Dilly
66850 (66577)	**CS**	CS	COLO	RU	David Maidment OBE

Class 66/9. Freightliner locos. Low emission "demonstrator" locos. Details as Class 66/0 except:

Engine: EMD 12N-710G3B-U2 two stroke of 2420 kW (3245 hp) at 904 rpm.
Traction Motors: General Motors D43TRC.
Fuel Capacity: 5905/5150 litres.

| 66951 | **FL** | E | DFHG | LD | |
| 66952 | **FL** | E | DFHG | LD | |

Class 66/9. Freightliner-operated low emission locos. Owing to the 665xx number range being full, subsequent deliveries of 66/5s were numbered from 66953 onwards. Details as Class 66/5 (low emission).

66953	**FL**	PC	DFHG	LD	
66954	**FL**	PC	DFIN	LD	
66955	**FL**	PC	DFIN	LD	
66956	**FL**	PC	DFHG	LD	
66957	**FL**	PC	DFHG	LD	Stephenson Locomotive Society 1909–2009

CLASS 67   ALSTOM/GENERAL MOTORS EMD Bo-Bo

Built: 1999–2000 by Alstom at Valencia, Spain, as sub-contractors for General Motors (General Motors model JT42 HW-HS).
Engine: GM 12N-710G3B-EC two stroke of 2385 kW (3200 hp) at 904 rpm.
Main Alternator: General Motors AR9A/HEP7/CA6C.
Traction Motors: General Motors D43FM.
Maximum Tractive Effort: 141 kN (31770 lbf).
Continuous Tractive Effort: 90 kN (20200 lbf) at 46.5 mph.
Power at Rail: 1860 kW.   **Train Brakes:** Air.

Brake Force: 78 t.
Weight: 90 t.
Design Speed: 125 mph.
Fuel Capacity: 4927 litres.
Train Supply: Electric, index 66.

Dimensions: 19.74 x 2.72 m.
Wheel Diameter: 965 mm.
Maximum Speed: 125 mph.
RA: 8.
Multiple Working: AAR System.

All equipped with Slow Speed Control and Swinghead Automatic "Buckeye" Combination Couplers.

67001/002/029 have been modified to operate in push-pull mode on the Arriva Trains Wales loco-hauled set.

67004, 67007, 67009 and 67011 are fitted with cast iron brake blocks for working the Fort William Sleeper. **Maximum Speed:** 80 mph.

67008/010/012–015/017/018/023/025 have been modified to operate in push-pull mode on the Chiltern Railways loco-hauled sets.

67013 carries its name on one side only.

Non-standard liveries: 67026 Diamond Jubilee silver.

67029 All over silver with DB logos.

67001	**AB**	A	WAWC	CE	
67002	**AB**	A	WAWC	CE	
67003	**AB**	A	WAAC	CE	
67004 r	**E**	A	WABC	CE	
67005	**RZ**	A	WAAC	CE	Queen's Messenger
67006	**RZ**	A	WAAC	CE	Royal Sovereign
67007 r	**E**	A	WABC	CE	
67008	**E**	A	WACC	CE	
67009 r	**E**	A	WABC	CE	
67010	**CM**	A	WACC	CE	
67011 r	**E**	A	WABC	CE	
67012	**CM**	A	WAWC	CE	A Shropshire Lad
67013	**CM**	A	WACC	CE	Dyfrbont Pontcysyllte
67014	**CM**	A	WACC	CE	Thomas Telford
67015	**CM**	A	WAAC	CE	David J. Lloyd
67016	**E**	A	WAAC	CE	
67017	**E**	A	WACC	CE	Arrow
67018	**DB**	A	WACC	CE	Keith Heller
67019	**E**	A	WAAC	CE	
67020	**E**	A	WAAC	CE	
67021	**E**	A	WAAC	CE	
67022	**E**	A	WACC	CE	
67023	**E**	A	WAAC	CE	
67024	**E**	A	WAAC	CE	
67025	**E**	A	WAAC	CE	Western Star
67026	**O**	A	WAAC	CE	Diamond Jubilee
67027	**DB**	A	WAAC	CE	
67028	**E**	A	WAAC	CE	
67029	**O**	A	WAAC	CE	Royal Diamond
67030 r	**E**	A	WABC	CE	

CLASS 68   VOSSLOH   Bo-Bo

New Vossloh mixed-traffic locos currently being delivered to DRS. 68010–015 will be dedicated to operating the Chiltern Railways loco-hauled trains.

Built: 2012–14 by Vossloh, Valencia, Spain.
Engine: Caterpillar C175-16 of 2800 kW (3750 hp) at 1740 rpm.
Main Alternator: ABB WGX560.
Traction Motors: 4 x AC frame mounted ABB 4FRA6063.
Maximum Tractive Effort: 317 kN (71 260 lbf).
Continuous Tractive Effort:

Power at Rail:	**Train Brakes:** Air.
Brake Force: 65.2 t.	**Dimensions:** 20.50 x 2.69 m.
Weight: 86 t.	**Wheel Diameter:** 1100 mm.
Design Speed: 100 mph.	**Maximum Speed:** 100 mph.
Fuel Capacity: 6000 litres.	**RA:** 7.
Train Supply: Electric, index 100.	

Multiple Working: Within class and with Class 88. 68008–015 AAR system.

68001	**DI**	PC	XHVE	CR	Evolution
68002	**DI**	PC	XHVE	CR	Intrepid
68003	**DI**	PC	XHVE	CR	Astute
68004	**DI**	PC	XHVE	CR	Rapid
68005	**DI**	PC	XHVE	CR	Defiant
68006	**DI**	PC	XHVE	CR	Daring
68007	**DI**	PC	XHVE	CR	Valiant
68008	**DI**	PC	XHVE	CR	Avenger
68009	**DI**	PC	XHVE	CR	Titan
68010	**CM**	PC	XHCE	CR	
68011	**CM**	PC	XHCE	CR	
68012	**CM**	PC	XHCE	CR	
68013	**CM**	PC	XHCE	CR	
68014	**CM**	PC	XHCE	CR	
68015	**CM**	PC	XHCE	CR	
68016		PC			
68017		PC			
68018		PC			
68019		PC			
68020		PC			
68021		PC			
68022		PC			
68023		PC			
68024		PC			
68025		PC			

CLASS 70   GENERAL ELECTRIC   Co-Co

New GE "PowerHaul" locomotives. 70012 was badly damaged whilst being unloaded in 2011 and was returned to Pennsylvania.

70801 (built as 70099) is a Turkish-built demonstrator that arrived in Britain in October 2012. Colas Rail leased this locomotive and then in 2013 ordered a further nine locomotives (70802–810) that were delivered in 2014.

Built: 2009–14 by General Electric, Erie, Pennsylvania, USA or by TÜLOMSAS, Eskişehir, Turkey (70801).
Engine: General Electric PowerHaul P616LDA1 of 2848 kW (3820 hp) at 1500 rpm.
Main Alternator: General Electric GTA series.
Traction Motors: AC-GE 5GEB30.
Maximum Tractive Effort: 544 kN (122 000 lbf).
Continuous Tractive Effort: 427 kN (96 000 lbf) at ?? m.p.h.

Power at Rail:
Brake Force: 96.7 t.
Weight: 129 t.
Design Speed: 75 mph.
Fuel Capacity: 6000 litres.
Train Supply: Not equipped.

Train Brakes: Air.
Dimensions: 21.71 x 2.64 m.
Wheel Diameter: 1066 mm.
Maximum Speed: 75 mph.
RA: 7.
Multiple Working: AAR System.

Class 70/0. Freightliner locos.

70001	**FH**	MQ	DFGI	LD	PowerHaul
70002	**FH**	MQ	DFGH	LD	
70003	**FH**	MQ	DFGH	LD	
70004	**FH**	MQ	DFGH	LD	The Coal Industry Society
70005	**FH**	MQ	DFGH	LD	
70006	**FH**	MQ	DFGH	LD	
70007	**FH**	MQ	DFGI	LD	
70008	**FH**	MQ	DFGI	LD	
70009	**FH**	MQ	DFGI	LD	
70010	**FH**	MQ	DFGH	LD	
70011	**FH**	MQ	DFGH	LD	
70013	**FH**	MQ	DFGI	LD	
70014	**FH**	MQ	DFGI	LD	
70015	**FH**	MQ	DFGI	LD	
70016	**FH**	MQ	DFGI	LD	
70017	**FH**	MQ	DFGI	LD	
70018	**FH**	MQ	DFGI	LD	
70019	**FH**	MQ	DFGI	LD	
70020	**FH**	MQ	DFGI	LD	

Class 70/8. Colas Rail locos.

70801	**CS**	LF	COLO	RU
70802	**CS**	LF	COLO	RU
70803	**CS**	LF	COLO	RU
70804	**CS**	LF	COLO	RU
70805	**CS**	LF	COLO	RU
70806	**CS**	LF	COLO	RU
70807	**CS**	LF	COLO	RU
70808	**CS**	LF	COLO	RU
70809	**CS**	LF	COLO	RU
70810	**CS**	LF	COLO	RU

2. ELECTRO-DIESEL &
ELECTRIC LOCOMOTIVES

CLASS 73   BR/ENGLISH ELECTRIC   Bo-Bo

Electro-diesel locomotives which can operate either from a DC supply or using power from a diesel engine.

Built: 1965–67 by English Electric Co. at Vulcan Foundry, Newton-le-Willows.
Engine: English Electric 4SRKT of 447 kW (600 hp) at 850 rpm.
Main Generator: English Electric 824/5D.
Electric Supply System: 750 V DC from third rail.
Traction Motors: English Electric 546/1B.
Maximum Tractive Effort (Electric): 179 kN (40000 lbf).
Maximum Tractive Effort (Diesel): 160 kN (36000 lbf).
Continuous Rating (Electric): 1060 kW (1420 hp) giving a tractive effort of 35 kN (7800 lbf) at 68 mph.
Continuous Tractive Effort (Diesel): 60 kN (13600 lbf) at 11.5 mph.
Maximum Rail Power (Electric): 2350 kW (3150 hp) at 42 mph.
Train Brakes: Air, vacuum & electro-pneumatic († Air & electro-pneumatic).
Brake Force: 31 t.   **Dimensions:** 16.36 x 2.64 m.
Weight: 77 t.   **Wheel Diameter:** 1016 mm.
Design Speed: 90 mph.   **Maximum Speed:** 90 mph.
Fuel Capacity: 1409 litres.   **RA:** 6.
Train Supply: Electric, index 66 (on electric power only).
Multiple Working: SR 27-way System & Blue Star.

Formerly numbered E6001–E6020/E6022–E6026/E6028–E6049 (not in order).

Locomotives numbered in the 732xx series are classed as 73/2 and were originally dedicated to Gatwick Express services.

Two separate rebuilt projects are underway. For GBRf at least ten locomotives are being rebuilt at Brush, Loughborough with an MTU R43 4000 V7 1600 hp engine (these will be renumbered in the 73961–970 series). For Network Rail 73104/211 are being rebuilt at RVEL, Derby with a pair of QSK19 750 hp engines (these will become 73951/952).

Non-standard liveries:

73107 Two-tone grey.
73109 Mid blue.
73139 Weardale Railway brown & cream.

73101	**PC**	RE	RVLO	ZA (S)	
73107	**0**	GB	GBED	SE	Redhill 1844–1994
73109	**0**	GB	GBED	SE	
73119	**B**	GB	GBED	SE	Borough of Eastleigh
73128	**E**	20	MBED	SE	
73133	**TT**	TT	MBED	BM	
73136	**GB**	GB	GBED	SE	

73138	**Y**	NR	QADD	ZA	
73139	**0**	RE	RVLO	ZA (S)	
73141	**GB**	GB	GBED	SE	Charlotte
73201 †	**B**	GB	GBED	SE	Broadlands
73202 †	**SN**	P	MBED	SL	
73207 †	**BL**	GB	GBED	SE	
73212 †	**GB**	GB	GBED	SE	Fiona
73213 †	**GB**	GB	GBED	SE	Rhodalyn
73235 †	**SD**	P	HYWD	BM	

The 7395x number series reserved for rebuilt Network Rail locomotives. Full details awaited.

73951 (73104)	**Y**	RE	RVLO	ZA (S)	
73952 (73211)	**Y**	RE	RVLO	ZA (S)	

The 7396x and 7397x number series reserved for rebuilt GBRf locomotives. Full details awaited.

73961 (73209)	**GB**	GB	GBBR	SE	
73962 (73204)	**GB**	GB	GBBR	SE	Dick Mabbutt
73963 (73206)		GB	GBBR	LB (S)	
73964 (73205)		GB	GBBR	LB (S)	
73965 (73208)		GB	GBBR	LB (S)	
73966 (73005)		GB	GBBR	LB (S)	
73967 (73006)		GB	GBBR	LB (S)	
73968 (73103)		GB	GBBR	BO (S)	
73969 (73105)		GB	GBBR	BO (S)	
73970 (73117)		GB	GBBR	BO (S)	

CLASS 86   BR/ENGLISH ELECTRIC   Bo-Bo

Built: 1965–66 by English Electric Co at Vulcan Foundry, Newton-le-Willows or by BR at Doncaster Works.
Electric Supply System: 25 kV AC 50 Hz overhead.
Train Brakes: Air.   **Brake Force:** 40 t.
Dimensions: 17.83 x 2.65 m.   **Weight:** 83–86.8 t.
RA: 6.   **Multiple Working:** TDM system.
Train Supply: Electric, index 66.

Formerly numbered E3101–E3200 (not in order).

Class 86s exported for use abroad are listed in section 6 of this book.

Class 86/1. Class 87-type bogies & motors.

Details as above except:
Traction Motors: GEC 412AZ frame mounted.
Maximum Tractive Effort: 258 kN (58000 lbf).
Continuous Rating: 3730 kW (5000 hp) giving a tractive effort of 95 kN (21300 lbf) at 87 mph.
Maximum Rail Power: 5860 kW (7860 hp) at 50.8 mph.
Wheel Diameter: 1150 mm.   **Weight:** 86.8 t.

Design Speed: 110 mph.   **Maximum Speed:** 110 mph.

| 86101 | **B** | EL | ACAC | | WN | Sir William A Stanier FRS |

Class 86/2. Standard design rebuilt with resilient wheels & Flexicoil suspension.

Traction Motors: AEI 282BZ axle hung.
Maximum Tractive Effort: 207 kN (46500 lbf).
Continuous Rating: 3010 kW (4040 hp) giving a tractive effort of 85 kN (19200 lbf) at 77.5 mph.
Maximum Rail Power: 4550 kW (6100 hp) at 49.5 mph.
Wheel Diameter: 1156 mm.   **Weight:** 85–86.2 t.
Design Speed: 125 mph.   **Maximum Speed:** 100 mph.

Non-standard livery: 86259 BR "Electric blue".

86229	**V**	EP	EPEX	LM (S)	
86231	**V**	EP	EPEX	LM (S)	
86234	**AR**	EP	EPEX	LM (S)	
86235	**AR**	EP	EPUK	LM (S)	
86246	**AR**	EP	EPEX	LM (S)	
86247	**EX**	P	DHLT	BA (S)	
86251	**V**	EP	EPEX	LM (S)	
86259 x	**0**	PP	MBEL	WN	Les Ross

Class 86/4.

Traction Motors: AEI 282AZ axle hung.
Maximum Tractive Effort: 258 kN (58000 lbf).
Continuous Rating: 2680 kW (3600 hp) giving a tractive effort of 89 kN (20000 lbf) at 67 mph.
Maximum Rail Power: 4400 kW (5900 hp) at 38 mph.
Wheel Diameter: 1156 mm.   **Weight:** 83–83.9 t.
Design Speed: 100 mph.   **Maximum Speed:** 100 mph.

| 86401 | **N** | EL | ACXX | | WN (S) Northampton Town |

Class 86/5. Regeared locomotive operated by Freightliner.

Details as Class 86/4 except:

Continuous Rating: 2680 kW (3600 hp) giving a tractive effort of 117 kN (26300 lbf) at 67 mph.
Maximum Speed: 75 mph.   **Train Supply:** Electric, isolated.

| 86501 (86608) | **FL** | FL | DFMC | CP | |

Class 86/6. Freightliner-operated locomotives.

Details as Class 86/4 except:

Maximum Speed: 75 mph.   **Train Supply:** Electric, isolated.

86604	**FL**	FL	DFNC	CP
86605	**FL**	FL	DFNC	CP
86607	**FL**	FL	DFNC	CP
86609	**FL**	FL	DFNC	CP
86610	**FL**	FL	DFNC	CP

86612	**FL**	P	DFNC	CP
86613	**FL**	P	DFNC	CP
86614	**FL**	P	DFNC	CP
86622	**FH**	P	DFNC	CP
86627	**FL**	P	DFNC	CP
86628	**FL**	P	DFNC	CP
86632	**FL**	P	DFNC	CP
86637	**FH**	P	DFNC	CP
86638	**FL**	P	DFNC	CP
86639	**FL**	P	DFNC	CP

Class 86/7. Europhoenix-owned locomotives. Refurbished Class 86/2s for the UK spot-hire market. Details as Class 86/2 unless stated.

Maximum Speed: 110 mph.   **Weight:** 85 t.
Train Supply: Electric, index 74.

| 86701 | (86205) | **CS** | EP | EPUK | WN (S) | Orion |
| 86702 | (86260) | **EL** | EP | EPUK | BH (S) | Cassiopeia |

CLASS 87   BREL/GEC   Bo-Bo

Built: 1973–75 by BREL at Crewe Works.
Electric Supply System: 25 kV AC 50 Hz overhead.
Traction Motors: GEC G412AZ frame mounted.
Maximum Tractive Effort: 258 kN (58000 lbf).
Continuous Rating: 3730 kW (5000 hp) giving a tractive effort of 95 kN (21300 lbf) at 87 mph.
Maximum Rail Power: 5860 kW (7860 hp) at 50.8 mph.
Train Brakes: Air.   **Brake Force:** 40 t.
Dimensions: 17.83 x 2.65 m.   **Weight:** 83.3 t.
Wheel Diameter: 1150 mm.   **Design Speed:** 110 mph.
Maximum Speed: 110 mph.   **Train Supply:** Electric, index 95.
RA: 6.   **Multiple Working:** TDM system.

Class 87s exported for use abroad are listed in section 6 of this book.

| 87002 | **B** | EL | ETLO | WN | Royal Sovereign |

CLASS 88   VOSSLOH   Bo-Bo

Ten new Vossloh bi-mode locomotives on order for DRS and due for delivery 2015–16. Full details awaited.
Built: 2014–15 by Vossloh, Valencia, Spain.
Electric Supply System: 25 kV AC 50 Hz overhead.
Engine: Caterpillar 12-cylinder 700 kW (940 hp) at 1800 rpm.
Traction Motors: ABB.
Maximum Tractive Effort (Electric):
Maximum Tractive Effort (Diesel):
Continuous Rating: 4000 kW (5360 hp).
Maximum Rail Power: **Dimensions:**
Train Brakes: Air.   **Brake Force:**
Weight: **Wheel Diameter:**

Fuel capacity:
Design Speed: 100 mph.
RA:

Train Supply:
Maximum Speed: 100 mph.

Multiple Working: Within class and with Class 68.

88001	PC
88002	PC
88003	PC
88004	PC
88005	PC
88006	PC
88007	PC
88008	PC
88009	PC
88010	PC

CLASS 90   GEC   Bo-Bo

Built: 1987–90 by BREL at Crewe Works (as sub contractors for GEC).
Electric Supply System: 25 kV AC 50 Hz overhead.
Traction Motors: GEC G412CY frame mounted.
Maximum Tractive Effort: 258 kN (58000 lbf).
Continuous Rating: 3730 kW (5000 hp) giving a tractive effort of 95 kN (21300 lbf) at 87 mph.
Maximum Rail Power: 5860 kW (7860 hp) at 68.3 mph.
Train Brakes: Air.
Brake Force: 40 t.
Weight: 84.5 t.
Design Speed: 110 mph.
Train Supply: Electric, index 95.
Multiple Working: TDM system.

Dimensions: 18.80 x 2.74 m.
Wheel Diameter: 1150 mm.
Maximum Speed: 110 mph.
RA: 7.

90001 b	**GA**	P	IANA	NC	Crown Point
90002 b	**1**	P	IANA	NC	Eastern Daily Press 1870–2010 SERVING NORFOLK FOR 140 YEARS
90003 b	**NX**	P	IANA	NC	Rædwald of East Anglia
90004 b	**1**	P	IANA	NC	City of Chelmsford
90005 b	**GA**	P	IANA	NC	Vice-Admiral Lord Nelson
90006 b	**1**	P	IANA	NC	Modern Railways Magazine/ Roger Ford
90007 b	**1**	P	IANA	NC	Sir John Betjeman
90008 b	**NX**	P	IANA	NC	The East Anglian
90009 b	**1**	P	IANA	NC	Diamond Jubilee
90010 b	**GA**	P	IANA	NC	
90011 b	**GA**	P	IANA	NC	East Anglian Daily Times Suffolk & Proud
90012 b	**1**	P	IANA	NC	Royal Anglian Regiment
90013 b	**GA**	P	IANA	NC	
90014 b	**GA**	P	IANA	NC	Norfolk and Norwich Festival
90015 b	**NX**	P	IANA	NC	Colchester Castle
90016	**FL**	P	DFLC	CP	
90017	**E**	DB	WQBA	CE (S)	

90018	DB	DB	WEAC	CE	
90019	FS	DB	WEAC	CE	
90020	E	DB	WEAC	CE	Collingwood
90021	FS	DB	WEAC	CE	
90022	EG	DB	WQBA	CE (S)	Freightconnection
90023	E	DB	WQBA	CE (S)	
90024	FS	DB	WEAC	CE	
90025	F	DB	WQBA	CE (S)	
90026	E	DB	WEAC	CE	
90027	F	DB	WQBA	CE (S)	Allerton T&RS Depot
90028	E	DB	WEAC	CE	
90029	DB	DB	WEAC	CE	
90030	E	DB	WQBA	CE (S)	
90031	E	DB	WQBA	CE (S)	The Railway Children Partnership Working For Street Children Worldwide
90032	E	DB	WQBA	CE (S)	
90033	FE	DB	WQBA	CE (S)	
90034	DR	DB	WEDC	CE	
90035	E	DB	WQAA	CE (S)	
90036	DB	DB	WEAC	CE	
90037	E	DB	WEAC	CE	Spirit of Dagenham
90038	FE	DB	WQBA	CE (S)	
90039	E	DB	WEAC	CE	
90040	E	DB	WQBA	CE (S)	The Railway Mission
90041	FL	P	DFLC	CP	
90042	FH	P	DFLC	CP	
90043	FF	P	DFLC	CP	Freightliner Coatbridge
90044	FF	P	DFLC	CP	
90045	FH	P	DFLC	CP	
90046	FL	P	DFLC	CP	
90047	FF	P	DFLC	CP	
90048	FF	P	DFLC	CP	
90049	FH	P	DFLC	CP	
90050	FF	AV	MBEL	CP (S)	

CLASS 91   GEC   Bo-Bo

Built: 1988–91 by BREL at Crewe Works (as sub contractors for GEC).
Electric Supply System: 25 kV AC 50 Hz overhead.
Traction Motors: GEC G426AZ.
Maximum Tractive Effort: 190 kN (43 000 lbf).
Continuous Rating: 4540 kW (6090 hp) giving a tractive effort of 170 kN at 96 mph.
Maximum Rail Power: 4700 kW (6300 hp) at ?? mph.
Train Brakes: Air.
Brake Force: 45 t.
Weight: 84 t.
Design Speed: 140 mph.
Train Supply: Electric, index 95.
Multiple Working: TDM system.
Dimensions: 19.41 x 2.74 m.
Wheel Diameter: 1000 mm.
Maximum Speed: 125 mph.
RA: 7.

Locomotives originally numbered in the 910xx series, but renumbered upon completion of overhauls at Bombardier, Doncaster by the addition of 100 to their original number. The exception to this rule was 91023 which was renumbered 91132.

91114 has been fitted with a second pantograph for evaluation purposes.

Non-standard/advertising liveries: 91101 Flying Scotsman (purple).

91110 Battle of Britain (black and grey).

91125 Sky 1 (blue).

91101	**AL**	E	IECA	BN	
91102	**EC**	E	IECA	BN	City of York
91103	**EC**	E	IECA	BN	
91104	**EC**	E	IECA	BN	
91105	**EC**	E	IECA	BN	
91106	**EC**	E	IECA	BN	
91107	**EC**	E	IECA	BN	SKYFALL
91108	**EC**	E	IECA	BN	
91109	**EC**	E	IECA	BN	Sir Bobby Robson
91110	**AL**	E	IECA	BN	BATTLE OF BRITAIN MEMORIAL FLIGHT
91111	**EC**	E	IECA	BN	
91112	**EC**	E	IECA	BN	
91113	**EC**	E	IECA	BN	
91114	**EC**	E	IECA	BN	Durham Cathedral
91115	**EC**	E	IECA	BN	Blaydon Races
91116	**EC**	E	IECA	BN	
91117	**EC**	E	IECA	BN	WEST RIDING LIMITED
91118	**EC**	E	IECA	BN	
91119	**EC**	E	IECA	BN	
91120	**EC**	E	IECA	BN	
91121	**EC**	E	IECA	BN	
91122	**EC**	E	IECA	BN	
91124	**EC**	E	IECA	BN	
91125	**AL**	E	IECA	BN	
91126	**EC**	E	IECA	BN	
91127	**EC**	E	IECA	BN	
91128	**EC**	E	IECA	BN	
91129	**EC**	E	IECA	BN	
91130	**EC**	E	IECA	BN	
91131	**EC**	E	IECA	BN	
91132	**EC**	E	IECA	BN	

CLASS 92   BRUSH   Co-Co

Built: 1993–96 by Brush Traction at Loughborough.
Electric Supply System: 25 kV AC 50 Hz overhead or 750 V DC third rail.
Traction Motors: Asea Brown Boveri design. Model 6FRA 7059B (Asynchronous 3-phase induction motors).
Maximum Tractive Effort: 400 kN (90 000 lbf).
Continuous Rating: 5040 kW (6760 hp) on AC, 4000 kW (5360 hp) on DC.

Maximum Rail Power:
Brake Force: 63 t.
Weight: 126 t.
Design Speed: 140 km/h (87 mph).
Train Supply: Electric, index 108 (AC), 70 (DC).
RA: 7.

Train Brakes: Air.
Dimensions: 21.34 x 2.67 m.
Wheel Diameter: 1070 mm.
Maximum Speed: 145 km/h (90 mph).

* Modified to operate freight trains on High Speed 1.

Class 92s exported for use abroad are listed in section 6 of this book.

Advertising livery: 92017 Stobart Rail (two-tone blue & white).

92002		**EG**	DB	WFAC	CE	H.G. Wells
92003	*	**EG**	DB	WFBC	CE	Beethoven
92004		**EG**	DB	WGEE	CE (S)	Jane Austen
92005	*	**EG**	DB	WFDC	CE	Mozart
92006		**EP**	GB	PTXX	LB (S)	Louis Armand
92007		**EG**	DB	WQBA	CE (S)	Schubert
92008		**EG**	DB	WQBA	CE (S)	Jules Verne
92009	*	**DB**	DB	WQBA	CE (S)	Marco Polo
92010		**EP**	GB	GBET	CO	Molière
92011		**EG**	DB	WFAC	CE	Handel
92013		**EG**	DB	WQAA	CE (S)	Puccini
92014		**EP**	GB	GBET	LB (S)	Emile Zola
92015	*	**DB**	DB	WFBC	CE	
92016	*	**DB**	DB	WFBC	CE	
92017		**AL**	DB	WQBA	CE (S)	Bart the Engine
92018		**EP**	GB	GBET	LB (S)	Stendhal
92019		**EG**	DB	WFBC	CE	Wagner
92020		**EP**	GB	PTXX	LB (S)	Milton
92021		**EP**	GB	PTXX	CO (S)	Purcell
92022		**EG**	DB	WQBA	CE (S)	Charles Dickens
92023		**EP**	GB	GBET	LB (S)	Ravel
92024		**EG**	DB	WQAA	CE (S)	J.S. Bach
92026		**EG**	DB	WQBA	CE (S)	Britten
92028		**EP**	GB	GBET	CO	Saint Saëns
92029		**EG**	DB	WFAC	CE	Dante
92030		**EG**	DB	WQAA	CE (S)	Ashford
92031	*	**DB**	DB	WFBC	CE	
92032		**GB**	GB	GBET	CO	IMechE Railway Division
92033		**EP**	GB	GBET	LB (S)	Berlioz
92035		**EP**	GB	WQBA	CE (S)	Mendelssohn
92036	*	**EG**	DB	WFBC	CE	Bertolt Brecht
92037		**EG**	DB	WFAC	CE	Sullivan
92038		**EP**	GB	GBET	CO	Voltaire
92039		**EG**	DB	WFCC	CE	Johann Strauss
92040		**EP**	GB	PTXX	CO (S)	Goethe
92041	*	**EG**	DB	WFAC	CE	Vaughan Williams
92042	*	**DB**	DB	WFBC	CE	
92043		**EP**	GB	GBET	CO	Debussy
92044		**EP**	GB	GBET	CO	Couperin
92045		**EP**	GB	GBET	LB (S)	Chaucer
92046		**EP**	GB	GBET	LB (S)	Sweelinck

3. EUROTUNNEL LOCOMOTIVES

DIESEL LOCOMOTIVES

0001–0007   MaK   Bo-Bo

Built: 1991–92 by MaK at Kiel, Germany (Model DE1004).
Engine: MTU 12V 396 TC13 of 940 kW (1260 hp) at 1800 rpm.
Main Alternator: ABB.   **Traction Motors:** ABB.
Maximum Tractive Effort: 305 kN (68600 lbf).
Continuous Tractive Effort: 140 kN (31500 lbf) at 20 mph.
Power At Rail: 750 kW (1012 hp).   **Dimensions:** 14.40 x ?? m.
Brake Force: 120 kN.   **Wheel Diameter:** 1000 mm.
Weight: 82 t.   **Maximum Speed:** 100 km/h.
Design Speed: 120 km/h.   **Train Brakes:** Air.
Fuel Capacity: 3500 litres.   **Multiple Working:** Within class.
Train Supply: Not equipped.   **Signalling System:** TVM430 cab signalling.

Registered on TOPS as 21901–907.

0001	**GY**	ET	CO
0002	**GY**	ET	CO
0003	**GY**	ET	CO
0004	**GY**	ET	CO
0005	**GY**	ET	CO

The following two locos were rebuilt from NS 6400 Class 6456 and 6457 (built 1991) and added to the Eurotunnel fleet in 2011.

0006	**GY**	ET	CO
0007	**GY**	ET	CO

0031–0042   HUNSLET/SCHÖMA   0-4-0

Built: 1989–90 by Hunslet Engine Company at Leeds as 900 mm gauge.
Rebuilt: 1993–94 by Schöma in Germany to 1435 mm gauge.
Engine: Deutz FL10L 413FW of 170 kW (230 hp) at 2300 rpm.
Transmission: Mechanical Clark 5000 series.
Maximum Tractive Effort:
Continuous Tractive Effort:
Power At Rail:
Brake Force: **Dimensions:** 6.63 x 2.69 m.
Weight: 26–28 t.   **Wheel Diameter:**
Design Speed: 48 km/h.   **Maximum Speed:** 50 km/h.
Fuel Capacity: **Train Brakes:** Air.
Train Supply: Not equipped.   **Multiple Working:** Not equipped.

* Rebuilt with inspection platforms to check overhead catenary.

0031	**GY**	ET	CO	FRANCES

0032		**GY**	ET	CO	ELISABETH
0033		**GY**	ET	CO	SILKE
0034		**GY**	ET	CO	AMANDA
0035		**GY**	ET	CO	MARY
0036		**GY**	ET	CO	LAURENCE
0037		**GY**	ET	CO	LYDIE
0038		**GY**	ET	CO	JENNY
0039	*	**GY**	ET	CO	PACITA
0040		**GY**	ET	CO	JILL
0041	*	**GY**	ET	CO	KIM
0042		**GY**	ET	CO	NICOLE

ELECTRIC LOCOMOTIVES

9005–9840 BRUSH/ABB Bo-Bo-Bo

Built: 1993–2002 by Brush Traction at Loughborough.
Supply System: 25 kV AC 50 Hz overhead.
Traction Motors: Asea Brown Boveri design. Asynchronous 3-phase motors. Model 6FHA 7059 (as built). Model 6FHA 7059C (7000 kW rated locos).
Maximum Tractive Effort: 400kN (90 000 lbf).
Continuous Rating: Class 9/0 and 9/1: 5760 kW (7725 hp). Class 9/7 and 9/8: 7000 kW (9387 hp).

Maximum Rail Power:	**Multiple Working:** TDM system.
Brake Force: 50 t.	**Dimensions:** 22.01 x 2.97 x 4.20 m.
Weight: 136 t.	**Wheel Diameter:** 1250 mm.
Design Speed: 100 mph.	**Maximum Speed:** 100 mph.
Train Supply: Electric.	**Train Brakes:** Air.

Class 9/0 Original build locos. Built 1993–94.

9005	**EB**	ET	CO	JESSYE NORMAN
9007	**EB**	ET	CO	DAME JOAN SUTHERLAND
9011	**EB**	ET	CO	JOSÉ VAN DAM
9013	**EB**	ET	CO	MARIA CALLAS
9015	**EB**	ET	CO	LÖTSCHBERG 1913
9018	**EB**	ET	CO	WILHELMENIA FERNANDEZ
9022	**EB**	ET	CO	DAME JANET BAKER
9024	**EB**	ET	CO	GOTTHARD 1882
9026	**EB**	ET	CO	FURKATUNNEL 1982
9029	**EB**	ET	CO	THOMAS ALLEN
9033	**EB**	ET	CO	MONTSERRAT CABALLE
9036	**EB**	ET	CO	ALAIN FONDARY
9037	**EB**	ET	CO	GABRIEL BACQUIER

Class 9/7. Increased power freight shuttle locos. Built 2001–02 (9711–23 built 1998–2001 as 9101–13 and rebuilt as 9711–23 2010–12).

9701	**EB**	ET	CO
9702	**EB**	ET	CO
9703	**EB**	ET	CO

9704	**EB**	ET	CO
9705	**EB**	ET	CO
9706	**EB**	ET	CO
9707	**EB**	ET	CO

9711	(9101)	**EB**	ET	CO
9712	(9102)	**EB**	ET	CO
9713	(9103)	**EB**	ET	CO
9714	(9104)	**EB**	ET	CO
9715	(9105)	**EB**	ET	CO
9716	(9106)	**EB**	ET	CO
9717	(9107)	**EB**	ET	CO
9718	(9108)	**EB**	ET	CO
9719	(9109)	**EB**	ET	CO
9720	(9110)	**EB**	ET	CO
9721	(9111)	**EB**	ET	CO
9722	(9112)	**EB**	ET	CO
9723	(9113)	**EB**	ET	CO

Class 9/8 Locos rebuilt from Class 9/0 by adding 800 to the loco number. Uprated to 7000 kW.

9801	**EB**	ET	CO		LESLEY GARRETT
9802	**EB**	ET	CO		STUART BURROWS
9803	**EB**	ET	CO		BENJAMIN LUXON
9804	**EB**	ET	CO		VICTORIA DE LOS ANGELES
9806	**EB**	ET	CO		REGINE CRESPIN
9808	**EB**	ET	CO		ELISABETH SODERSTROM
9809	**EB**	ET	CO		FRANÇOISE POLLET
9810	**EB**	ET	CO		JEAN-PHILIPPE COURTIS
9812	**EB**	ET	CO		LUCIANO PAVAROTTI
9814	**EB**	ET	CO		LUCIA POPP
9816	**EB**	ET	CO		WILLARD WHITE
9817	**EB**	ET	CO	(S)	JOSÉ CARRERAS
9819	**EB**	ET	CO		MARIA EWING
9820	**EB**	ET	CO		NICOLAI GHIAROV
9821	**EB**	ET	CO		TERESA BERGANZA
9823	**EB**	ET	CO		DAME ELISABETH LEGGE-SCHWARZKOPF
9825	**EB**	ET	CO		
9827	**EB**	ET	CO		BARBARA HENDRICKS
9828	**EB**	ET	CO		DAME KIRI TE KANAWA
9831	**EB**	ET	CO		
9832	**EB**	ET	CO		RENATA TEBALDI
9834	**EB**	ET	CO		MIRELLA FRENI
9835	**EB**	ET	CO		NICOLAI GEDDA
9838	**EB**	ET	CO		HILDEGARD BEHRENS
9840	**EB**	ET	CO		

▲ Colas Rail-liveried 60087 exits Chipping Sodbury Tunnel with 6V62 11.22 Tilbury–Llanwern steel empties on 06/08/14. **Jamie Squibbs**

▼ DRS-liveried 66303 is seen stabled at Crewe Gresty Bridge depot on 11/03/14. **Robert Pritchard**

▲ GBRf-liveried 66738 heads north at Slindon, Staffordshire, with 4F01 16.07 Ironbridge–Seaforth empty biomass as Pendolino 390 107 overtakes with the 16.07 London Euston–Liverpool Lime Street on 14/05/14. **Brad Joyce**

▲ Diamond Jubilee silver-liveried 67026 passes Inverkeithing East Jn with the 18.14 Glenrothes–Edinburgh ScotRail loco-hauled train on 09/07/14. **Ian Lothian**

▼ One of the new Vossloh Class 68s, 68006, stands at Inverness container terminal on 25/08/14. DRS has ordered 25 of these locomotives which carry the latest DRS livery. **Alexander Colley**

▲ Colas Rail-liveried 70803 (on hire to Freightliner) passes Bentley, Suffolk with 4M81 08.01 Felixstowe–Crewe Intermodal on 12/08/14. **Antony Guppy**

▼ Network Rail yellow-liveried 73138 trails a Crewe–Derby test train (led by 73141) at Longport on 25/07/14. **Cliff Beeton**

▲ The first of the rebuilt GBRf Class 73s, 73961, is seen on test at Quorn & Woodhouse on the Great Central Railway with preserved Class 31 D5830 on 17/09/14. **Keith Satterly**

▼ BR Blue-liveried 87002 passes Cromwell, between Retford and Newark, with an 07.09 Newcastle–London King's Cross GBRf charter on 09/08/14. **Lindsay Atkinson**

▲ Freightliner-liveried 86632 and 86609 pass Ashton, south of Roade, with 4L89 04.10 Crewe–Felixstowe intermodal on 16/07/14.

Nigel Gibbs

▲ Abellio Greater Anglia-liveried 90010 passes Ardleigh with the 12.00 Norwich–London Liverpool Street on 24/07/14. **Antony Guppy**

▼ Carrying the special Flying Scotsman purple livery, 91101 stands at York with the 15.00 London King's Cross–Edinburgh on 06/06/13. **Robert Pritchard**

▲ DB Schenker-liveried 92016 passes Botany Bay, north of Retford, with a diverted Daventry–Mossend intermodal on 25/05/14.　　**Andrew Mason**

▼ Eurotunnel Class 9/8 shuttle locomotive 9810 is seen stabled between duties at Coquelles depot in France on 27/02/14.　　**David Haydock**

4. FORMER BR MAIN LINE LOCOS IN INDUSTRIAL SERVICE

Former British Rail main line locomotives considered to be in "industrial use" are listed here. These locomotives do not currently have Network Rail engineering acceptance for operation on the national railway network.

Number Other no./name   Location

Class 03

Number	Other no./name	Location
03084	HELEN-LOUISE	West Coast Railway Company, Carnforth
03179	CLIVE	First Capital Connect, Hornsey Depot, London
03196	JOYCE/GLYNIS	West Coast Railway Company, Carnforth
D2381		West Coast Railway Company, Carnforth

Class 07

Number	Other no./name	Location
D2991	07007	Arlington Fleet Services, Eastleigh Works, Hampshire

Class 08

Number	Other no./name	Location
08202	CHUFFER	Chasewater Light Railway, Brownhills, Staffordshire
08308	23	PD Ports, Teesport, Grangetown, Middlesbrough
08331		Midland Railway-Butterley, Derbyshire
08375	21	Hanson Cement, Ketton Cement Works, nr Stamford
08389		Barrow Hill Roundhouse, Chesterfield, Derbyshire
08393		LH Group, Barton-under-Needwood, Staffordshire
08401		Celsa Steel (UK), Castle Works, Cardiff
08411		Colne Valley Railway, Halstead, Essex
08418		West Coast Railway Company, Carnforth
08423	H011 14	PD Ports, Teesport, Grangetown, Middlesbrough
08441		RSS, Rye Farm, Wishaw, Sutton Coldfield
08442	RICHARD J. WENHAM EASTLEIGH DEPOT	LNWR, Eastleigh Depot, Hampshire
08445		Daventry International Railfreight Terminal, Crick
08447		John G Russell (Transport), Hillington, Glasgow
08460		RSS, Rye Farm, Wishaw, Sutton Coldfield
08484	CAPTAIN NATHANIEL DARELL	RSS, Rye Farm, Wishaw, Sutton Coldfield
08485		West Coast Railway Company, Carnforth
08499		Colas Rail, Canton Depot, Cardiff
08502		Barrow Hill Roundhouse, Chesterfield, Derbyshire
08503		Barry Island Railway, Vale of Glamorgan
08507		Riviera Trains, Crewe Down Holding Sidings
08511		Felixstowe Dock & Railway Company, Felixstowe
08516		LNWR, Barton Hill Depot, Bristol
08527		Northern, Allerton Depot, Liverpool
08536		RVEL, RTC Business Park, Derby
08568	St. Rollox	Knorr-Bremse Rail Systems, Springburn Depot, Glasgow
08573		Bombardier Transportation, Ilford Works, London
08588		Cemex UK, Washwood Heath, Birmingham
08598	H016 HERCULES	Chasewater Light Railway, Brownhills, Staffordshire

08600		AV Dawson, Ayrton Rail Terminal, Middlesbrough
08602	004 BOMBER	Bombardier Transportation, Derby Works
08613	H064	Celtic Energy, Onllwyn Coal & Distribution Centre, West Glamorgan
08622	H028 19	Hanson Cement, Ketton Cement Works, nr Stamford
08629	Wolverton	Knorr-Bremse Rail Systems, Wolverton Works, Milton Keynes
08643		Aggregate Industries, Merehead Rail Terminal
08648	"08624"	PD Ports, Teesport, Grangetown, Middlesbrough
08649	Bradwell	Knorr-Bremse Rail Systems, Wolverton Works, Milton Keynes
08650	ISLE OF GRAIN	Bardon Aggregates, Isle of Grain, Kent
08652		Hanson Aggregates, Whatley Quarry, near Frome
08670		RSS, Rye Farm, Wishaw, Sutton Coldfield
08678	ARTILA	West Coast Railway Company, Carnforth
08682	Lionheart	Bombardier Transportation, Derby Works
08683		RSS, Rye Farm, Wishaw, Sutton Coldfield
08685		Barrow Hill Roundhouse, Chesterfield, Derbyshire
08699		Weardale Railway, Wolsingham, County Durham
08700		Barrow Hill Roundhouse, Chesterfield, Derbyshire
08704	D3871	Riviera Trains, Crewe Down Holding Sidings
08730	The Caley	Knorr-Bremse Rail Systems, Springburn Depot, Glasgow
08743	Bryan Turner	SembCorp Utilities Teesside, Wilton, Middlesbrough
08750		Weardale Railway, Wolsingham, County Durham
08756		Tata Steel, Shotton Works, Deeside, Flintshire
08762		Cemex UK, Washwood Heath, Birmingham
08764		Stonebridge Park Heavy Repair depot, Wembley, London
08765		Nemesis Rail, Burton-upon-Trent, Staffordshire
08774	ARTHUR VERNON DAWSON	AV Dawson, Ayrton Rail Terminal, Middlesbrough
08786		Barrow Hill Roundhouse, Chesterfield, Derbyshire
08787	08296	Hanson Aggregates, Machen Quarry, nr Newport
08807		AV Dawson, Ayrton Rail Terminal, Middlesbrough
08809	24	PD Ports, Teesport, Grangetown, Middlesbrough
08810		Northern, Heaton Depot, Newcastle
08818	MOLLY	GB Railfreight, Trafford Park Euroterminal, Gtr Manchester
08823	LIBBIE	Daventry International Railfreight Terminal, Crick
08834		Bombardier Transportation, Old Dalby Test Centre, Asfordby
08846	003	Bombardier Transportation, Derby Works
08868		LNWR, Crewe Carriage Depot, Crewe, Cheshire
08870	H024	Weardale Railway, Wolsingham, County Durham
08871	22	Weardale Railway, Wolsingham, County Durham
08873		Hams Hall Distribution Park, Coleshill, Warwickshire
08885	H042 18	Weardale Railway, Wolsingham, County Durham
08892		First Capital Connect, Hornsey Depot, London
08903	JOHN W. ANTILL	SembCorp Utilities Teesside, Wilton, Middlesbrough
08905		Hope Construction Materials, Hope Cement Works, Derbyshire
08912		AV Dawson, Ayrton Rail Terminal, Middlesbrough
08913		LH Group, Barton-under-Needwood, Staffordshire
08918		Nemesis Rail, Burton-upon-Trent, Staffordshire
08924	1	GB Railfreight, Garston Car Terminal, Liverpool
08927	D4157	EMD, Roberts Road Depot, Doncaster
08933		Aggregate Industries, Merehead Rail Terminal

08936		Tata Steel, Shotton Works, Deeside, Flintshire
08937	D4167	
	BLUEBELL MEL	Bardon Aggregates, Meldon Quarry, near Okehampton
08943		Bombardier Transportation, Central Rivers Depot, Barton-under-Needwood
08947	HOWIE	Arlington Fleet Services, Eastleigh Works, Hampshire
08956		Bombardier Transportation, Old Dalby Test Centre, Asfordby

Class 09

09007	D3671	London Overground, Willesden Depot, London
09014		Nemesis Rail, Burton-upon-Trent, Staffordshire
09022		Victoria Group, Port of Boston, Boston
09204		LNWR, Crewe Carriage Depot, Crewe, Cheshire

Class 14

D9504		Kent & East Sussex Railway
D9529	14029	Nene Valley Railway

Class 20

20056	81	Tata Steel, Appleby-Frodingham Works, Scunthorpe
20066	82	Tata Steel, Appleby-Frodingham Works, Scunthorpe
20121		Barrow Hill Roundhouse, Chesterfield, Derbyshire
20166		Rail Restorations North East, Shildon
20168	2 SIR GEORGE EARLE	Hope Construction Materials, Hope Cement Works, Derbyshire
20906	3	Hope Construction Materials, Hope Cement Works, Derbyshire

Class 47

47703		Wabtec Rail, Doncaster Works
47714		Bombardier Transportation, Old Dalby Test Centre, Asfordby

5. LOCOMOTIVES AWAITING DISPOSAL

Locomotives that are still extant but at scrapyards are listed here.

Class 08

08646	F	European Metal Recycling, Kingsbury
08783	E	European Metal Recycling, Kingsbury
08798	E	European Metal Recycling, Attercliffe
08872	E	European Metal Recycling, Attercliffe
08921	E	European Metal Recycling, Kingsbury

Class 09

09023	E	European Metal Recycling, Attercliffe
09107	E	European Metal Recycling, Kingsbury

Class 31

31410	RR	CF Booth, Rotherham

Class 86

86901	Y	CF Booth, Rotherham
86902	Y	CF Booth, Rotherham

6. LOCOMOTIVES EXPORTED FOR USE ABROAD

This section details former BR (plus privatisation era) diesel and electric locomotives that have been exported from the UK for use in industrial locations or by a main line operator abroad. Not included are locos that are "preserved" abroad, which are included in our "Preserved Locomotives of British Railways" publication. (S) denotes locomotives that are stored.

Number Other no./name   Location

Class 04

D2289		Lonato SpA, Lonato Steelworks, Lonato, Brescia, Italy

Class 56

56101	0659 001-5	FLOYD, Hungary
56115	0659 002-3	FLOYD, Hungary
56117	0659 003-1	FLOYD, Hungary

Class 58

58001		Axiom Rail, France, (S) Alizay
58004		Axiom Rail, France, (S) Alizay
58005		Axiom Rail, France, (S) Alizay
58006		Axiom Rail, France, (S) Alizay
58007		Axiom Rail, France, (S) Alizay
58009		Axiom Rail, France, (S) Alizay
58010		Axiom Rail, France, (S) Alizay
58011		Axiom Rail, France, (S) Alizay
58013		Axiom Rail, France, (S) Alizay
58015		Transfesa, Spain, (S) Monforte del Cid, Alicante
58018		Axiom Rail, France, (S) Alizay
58020	L43	Transfesa, Spain, (S) Monforte del Cid, Alicante
58021		Axiom Rail, France, (S) Alizay
58024	L42	Transfesa, Spain, (S) Monforte del Cid, Alicante
58025		DB Schenker, Spain, (S) Albacete
58026		Axiom Rail, France, (S) Alizay
58027	L52	DB Schenker, Spain, (S) Albacete
58029	L44	Transfesa, Spain, (S) Monforte del Cid, Alicante
58030	L46	Transfesa, Spain, (S) Monforte del Cid, Alicante
58031	L45	Transfesa, Spain, (S) Monforte del Cid, Alicante
58032		Axiom Rail, France, (S) Alizay
58033		Axiom Rail, France, (S) Alizay
58034		Axiom Rail, France, (S) Alizay
58035		Axiom Rail, France, (S) Alizay
58036		Axiom Rail, France, (S) Alizay
58038		Axiom Rail, France, (S) Alizay
58039		Axiom Rail, France, (S) Alizay
58040		Axiom Rail, France, (S) Alizay
58041	L36	Transfesa, Spain, (S) Albacete

58042		Axiom Rail, France, (S) Alizay
58043	L37	Transfesa, Spain, (S) Monforte del Cid, Alicante
58044		Axiom Rail, France, (S) Woippy, Metz
58046		Axiom Rail, France, (S) Alizay
58047	L51	Transfesa, Spain, (S) Monforte del Cid, Alicante
58049		Axiom Rail, France, (S) Alizay
58050	L53	DB Schenker, Spain, (S) Albacete

Class 66

66010	Euro Cargo Rail, France
66022	Euro Cargo Rail, France
66026	Euro Cargo Rail, France
66028	Euro Cargo Rail, France
66029	Euro Cargo Rail, France
66032	Euro Cargo Rail, France
66033	Euro Cargo Rail, France
66036	Euro Cargo Rail, France
66038	Euro Cargo Rail, France
66042	Euro Cargo Rail, France
66045	Euro Cargo Rail, France
66049	Euro Cargo Rail, France
66052	Euro Cargo Rail, France
66062	Euro Cargo Rail, France
66064	Euro Cargo Rail, France
66071	Euro Cargo Rail, France
66072	Euro Cargo Rail, France
66073	Euro Cargo Rail, France
66123	Euro Cargo Rail, France
66146	DB Schenker Rail Polska, Poland
66153	DB Schenker Rail Polska, Poland
66157	DB Schenker Rail Polska, Poland
66159	DB Schenker Rail Polska, Poland
66163	DB Schenker Rail Polska, Poland
66166	DB Schenker Rail Polska, Poland
66173	DB Schenker Rail Polska, Poland
66178	DB Schenker Rail Polska, Poland
66179	Euro Cargo Rail, France
66180	DB Schenker Rail Polska, Poland
66189	DB Schenker Rail Polska, Poland
66190	Euro Cargo Rail, France
66191	Euro Cargo Rail, France
66195	Euro Cargo Rail, France
66196	DB Schenker Rail Polska, Poland
66202	Euro Cargo Rail, France
66203	Euro Cargo Rail, France
66205	Euro Cargo Rail, France
66208	Euro Cargo Rail, France
66209	Euro Cargo Rail, France
66210	Euro Cargo Rail, France
66211	Euro Cargo Rail, France
66212	Euro Cargo Rail, France

66214		Euro Cargo Rail, France
66215		Euro Cargo Rail, France
66216		Euro Cargo Rail, France
66217		Euro Cargo Rail, France
66218		Euro Cargo Rail, France
66219		Euro Cargo Rail, France
66220		DB Schenker Rail Polska, Poland
66222		Euro Cargo Rail, France
66223		Euro Cargo Rail, France
66224		Euro Cargo Rail, France
66225		Euro Cargo Rail, France
66226		Euro Cargo Rail, France
66227		DB Schenker Rail Polska, Poland
66228		Euro Cargo Rail, France
66229		Euro Cargo Rail, France
66231		Euro Cargo Rail, France
66233		Euro Cargo Rail, France
66234		Euro Cargo Rail, France
66235		Euro Cargo Rail, France
66236		Euro Cargo Rail, France
66237		DB Schenker Rail Polska, Poland
66239		Euro Cargo Rail, France
66240		Euro Cargo Rail, France
66241		Euro Cargo Rail, France
66242		Euro Cargo Rail, France
66243		Euro Cargo Rail, France
66244		Euro Cargo Rail, France
66245		Euro Cargo Rail, France
66246		Euro Cargo Rail, France
66247		Euro Cargo Rail, France
66248		DB Schenker Rail Polska, Poland
66249		Euro Cargo Rail, France
66411	66013	Freightliner, Poland
66412	66015	Freightliner, Poland
66417	66014	Freightliner, Poland
66582	66009	Freightliner, Poland
66583	66010	Freightliner, Poland
66584	66011	Freightliner, Poland
66586	66008	Freightliner, Poland
66608	66603	Freightliner, Poland
66609	66604	Freightliner, Poland
66611	66605	Freightliner, Poland
66612	66606	Freightliner, Poland
66624	66602	Freightliner, Poland
66625	66601	Freightliner, Poland

Class 86

86215	91 55 0450 005-8	FLOYD, Hungary
86217	91 55 0450 006-6	FLOYD, Hungary
86218	91 55 0450 004-1	FLOYD, Hungary

86228	91 55 0450 007-4	FLOYD, Hungary
86232	91 55 0450 003-3	FLOYD, Hungary
86233		Bulmarket, Bulgaria (S)
86242	91 55 0450 008-2	FLOYD, Hungary
86248	91 55 0450 001-7	FLOYD, Hungary
86250	91 55 0450 002-5	FLOYD, Hungary
86424	91 55 0450 009-0	FLOYD, Hungary (S)

Class 87

87003	87003-0	BZK, Bulgaria
87004	87004-8 Britannia	BZK, Bulgaria
87006	87006-3	BZK, Bulgaria
87007	87007-1	BZK, Bulgaria
87008	87008-9	BZK, Bulgaria (S)
87009		Bulmarket, Bulgaria
87010	87010-5	BZK, Bulgaria
87012	87012-1	BZK, Bulgaria
87013	87013-9	BZK, Bulgaria
87014	87014-7	BZK, Bulgaria (S)
87017	Iron Duke	Bulmarket, Bulgaria
87019	87019-6	BZK, Bulgaria
87020	87020-4	BZK, Bulgaria
87022	87022-0	BZK, Bulgaria
87023	Velocity	Bulmarket, Bulgaria
87025		Bulmarket, Bulgaria
87026	87026-1	BZK, Bulgaria
87028	87028-7	BZK, Bulgaria
87029	87029-5	BZK, Bulgaria
87033	87033-7	BZK, Bulgaria
87034	87034-5	BZK, Bulgaria

Class 92

92001	91 53 0472 002-1 Mircea Eliade	DB Schenker, Romania
92012	91 53 0472 001-3 Mihai Eminescu	DB Schenker, Romania
92025	Oscar Wilde	DB Schenker, Bulgaria
92027	George Eliot	DB Schenker, Bulgaria
92034	Kipling	DB Schenker, Bulgaria

7. CODES

7.1. LIVERY CODES

Livery codes are used to denote the various liveries carried. It is impossible to list every livery variation which currently exists, in particular items ignored for this publication include:

- Minor colour variations.
- Omission of logos.
- All numbering, lettering and brandings.

Descriptions quoted are thus a general guide only. Logos as appropriate for each livery are normally deemed to be carried. The colour of the lower half of the bodyside is stated first.

1	"One" (metallic grey with a broad black bodyside stripe. White National Express/Greater Anglia "interim" stripe as branding).
AB	Arriva Trains Wales/Welsh Government sponsored dark blue.
AI	Aggregate Industries (green, light grey & blue).
AL	Advertising/promotional livery (see class heading for details).
AR	Anglia Railways (turquoise blue with a white stripe).
AZ	Advenza Freight (deep blue with green Advenza brandings).
B	BR blue.
BB	Balfour Beatty Rail (white & blue).
BL	BR Revised blue with yellow cabs, grey roof, large numbers & logo.
CD	Cotswold Rail (silver with blue & red logo).
CE	BR Civil Engineers (yellow & grey with black cab doors & window surrounds).
CM	Chiltern Mainline loco-hauled (two-tone grey & silver with blue stripes).
CS	Colas Rail (yellow, orange & black).
CU	Corus (silver with red logos).
DB	DB Schenker (Deutsche Bahn red with grey roof and solebar).
DC	Devon & Cornwall Railways (metallic silver).
DG	BR Departmental (dark grey with black cab doors & window surrounds).
DI	New DRS {Class 68 style} (deep blue & aquamarine with large compass logo).
DR	Direct Rail Services (dark blue with light blue or dark grey roof).
DS	Revised Direct Rail Services (dark blue, light blue & green. "Compass" logo).
E	English Welsh & Scottish Railway (maroon bodyside & roof with a broad gold bodyside band).
EB	Eurotunnel (two-tone grey with a broad blue stripe).
EC	East Coast (silver or grey with a purple stripe).
ECR	Euro Cargo Rail (light grey).
EG	"EWS grey" (as **F** but with large yellow & red EWS logo).
EL	Electric Traction Limited (silver & red).
EP	European Passenger Services (two-tone grey with dark blue roof).
EX	Europhoenix (silver, blue & red).
F	BR Trainload Freight (two-tone grey with black cab doors & window surrounds. Various logos).

FA Fastline Freight (grey & black with white & orange stripes).
FB First Group dark blue.
FE Railfreight Distribution International (two tone-grey with black cab doors & dark blue roof).
FER Fertis (light grey with a dark grey roof & solebar).
FF Freightliner grey (two-tone grey with black cab doors & window surrounds. Freightliner logo).
FH Revised Freightliner {PowerHaul} (dark green with yellow ends & a grey stripe/buffer beam).
FL Freightliner (dark green with yellow cabs).
FO BR Railfreight (grey bodysides, yellow cabs & red lower bodyside stripe, large BR logo).
FR Fragonset Railways (black with silver roof & a red bodyside band lined out in white).
FS First Group (indigo blue with pink & white stripes).
FY Foster Yeoman (blue & silver. Cast numberplates).
G BR Green (plain green, with white stripe on main line locomotives).
GA Abellio Greater Anglia (white with a black stripe).
GB GB Railfreight (blue with orange cantrail & solebar stripes, orange cabs).
GC Grand Central (all over black with an orange stripe).
GG BR green (two-tone green).
GIF GIF (Spain) light blue with a dark blue band.
GL First Great Western locomotives (green with a gold stripe (no gold stripe on shunters)).
GW Great Western Railway (green, lined out in black & orange).
GY Eurotunnel (grey & yellow).
HA Hanson Quarry Products (dark blue/silver with oxide red roof).
HN Harry Needle Railroad Company (orange with a black roof and solebar).
IC BR InterCity (dark grey/white/red/white).
K Black.
LH BR Loadhaul (black with orange cabsides).
LM London Midland (white/grey & green with broad black stripe around windows).
M BR maroon.
ML BR Mainline Freight (aircraft blue with a silver stripe).
N BR Network SouthEast (white & blue with red lower bodyside stripe, grey solebar & cab ends).
NX National Express (white with grey ends).
O Non-standard (see class heading for details).
PC Pullman Car Company (umber & cream with gold lettering lined out in gold).
RB Riviera Trains Oxford blue.
RG BR Parcels (dark grey & red).
RP Royal Train (claret, lined out in red & black).
RR Regional Railways (dark blue & grey with light blue & white stripes, three narrow dark blue stripes at vehicle ends).
RS RMS Locotec blue.
RX Rail Express Systems (dark grey & red with or without blue markings).
RZ Royal Train revised (plain claret, no lining).
SD South West Trains outer suburban {Class 450 style} (deep blue, orange & red).
SL Silverlink (indigo blue with white stripe, green lower body & yellow doors).

SN	Southern (white & dark green with light green semi-circles at one end of each vehicle. Light grey band at solebar level).
ST	Stagecoach (blue with red cabs).
TT	Transmart Trains (all over green).
U	White or grey undercoat.
V	Virgin Trains (red with black doors extending into bodysides, three white lower bodyside stripes).
VN	Belmond Northern Belle (crimson lake & cream lined out in gold).
VP	Virgin Trains shunters (black with a large black & white chequered flag on the bodyside).
WA	Wabtec Rail (black).
WC	West Coast Railway Company maroon.
XC	CrossCountry (two-tone silver with deep crimson ends and pink doors).
Y	Network Rail yellow.

7.2. OWNER CODES

Locomotives and rolling stock are owned by various companies and private owners and are allotted codes as follows:

20	Class 20189
40	Class 40 Preservation Society
47	Stratford 47 Group
50	Class 50 Alliance
56	Class 56 Locomotives
70	7029 Clun Castle
71	71A Locomotives
2L	Class Twenty Locomotives
A	Angel Trains
AI	Aggregate Industries
AM	Alstom
AV	Arriva UK Trains
BA	British American Railway Services
CS	Colas Rail
DB	DB Schenker Rail (UK)
DP	Deltic Preservation Society
DR	Direct Rail Services
DT	The Diesel Traction Group
E	Eversholt Rail (UK)
EL	Electric Traction Limited
EM	East Midlands Trains
EP	Europhoenix
ET	Eurotunnel
EU	Eurostar International
FG	First Group
FL	Freightliner
FW	First Great Western (assets of the Greater Western franchise)
GB	GB Railfreight
HA	The Hanson Group
HJ	Howard Johnston
HN	Harry Needle Railroad Company

LF	Lombard Finance
LM	London Midland
MQ	Macquarie Group
MW	Martin Walker
NB	Neil Boden
NM	National Museum of Science & Industry
NR	Network Rail
NS	Nemesis Rail
NY	North Yorkshire Moors Railway Enterprises
P	Porterbrook Leasing Company
PC	Pamplona Capital Management
PP	Peter Pan Locomotive Company
RE	Railway Vehicle Engineering
RL	Rail Management Services (trading as RMS Locotec)
RV	Riviera Trains
SN	Southern
TT	Transmart Trains
UR	UK Rail Leasing
WA	Wabtec Rail Group
WC	West Coast Railway Company

7.3. LOCOMOTIVE POOL CODES

Locomotives are split into operational groups ("pools") for diagramming and maintenance purposes. The official codes used to denote these pools are shown in this publication.

ACAC	Electric Traction Limited locomotives
ACXX	Electric Traction Limited locomotives for static depot use.
ATLO	Alstom Class 08.
AWCA	West Coast Railway Company operational locomotives.
AWCX	West Coast Railway Company stored locomotives.
CFOL	Class 50 Operations locomotives.
COFS	Colas Rail Class 56.
COLO	Colas Rail Classes 47, 60, 66 & 70.
COLS	Colas Rail stored locomotives.
COTS	Colas Rail Class 37.
DFGH	Freightliner Heavy Haul Class 70.
DFGI	Freightliner Intermodal Class 70.
DFHG	Freightliner Heavy Haul low emission Class 66.
DFHH	Freightliner Heavy Haul Class 66.
DFIM	Freightliner Intermodal Class 66.
DFIN	Freightliner Intermodal low emission Class 66.
DFLC	Freightliner Intermodal Class 90.
DFLH	Freightliner Heavy Haul Class 47.
DFLS	Freightliner Class 08.
DFMC	Freightliner Intermodal Class 86/5.
DFNC	Freightliner Intermodal Class 86/6.
DHLT	Freightliner locomotives awaiting maintenance/repair/disposal.
EFOO	First Great Western Class 57.

EFPC	First Great Western Class 43.
EFSH	First Great Western Class 08.
EHPC	CrossCountry Class 43.
EJLO	London Midland Class 08.
ELRD	East Lancashire Railway-based main line registered locomotives.
EMPC	East Midlands Trains Class 43.
EMSL	East Midlands Trains Class 08.
EPEX	Europhoenix locomotives for export.
EPUK	Europhoenix UK locomotives.
ETLO	Electric Traction Limited Class 87.
GBBR	GB Railfreight Class 73/9.
GBCM	GB Railfreight Class 66. General.
GBDF	GB Railfreight Class 47.
GBDR	GB Railfreight Class 66. Locomotives from Germany.
GBED	GB Railfreight Class 73.
GBEE	GB Railfreight Class 20. On hire from Harry Needle/Class 20189.
GBET	GB Railfreight Class 92.
GBFM	GB Railfreight Class 66. RETB fitted.
GBNB	GB Railfreight Class 66. New build.
GBNL	GB Railfreight Class 66. Locomotives from the Netherlands.
GBRT	GB Railfreight Class 66. Network Rail duties.
GBSD	GB Railfreight Class 66.
GBWM	GB Railfreight Class 08/09.
GBYH	GB Railfreight Class 59.
GCHP	Grand Central Class 43.
GPSS	Eurostar (UK) Class 08.
HBSH	Wabtec hire shunting locomotives.
HNRL	Harry Needle Railroad Company hire locomotives.
HNRS	Harry Needle Railroad Company stored locomotives.
HTLX	British American Railway Services locomotives.
HWSU	Southern Class 09.
HYWD	South West Trains Class 73.
IANA	Greater Anglia Class 90.
IECA	East Coast Class 91.
IECP	East Coast Class 43.
MBDL	Non TOC-owned diesel locomotives.
MBED	Non TOC-owned electro-diesel locomotives.
MBEL	Non TOC-owned electric locomotives.
MOLO	Class 20189 Ltd Class 20s.
MRSO	RMS Locotec Class 08.
NRLO	Nemesis Rail locomotives.
PTXX	GB Railfreight Class 92 (stored).
QADD	Network Rail diesel locomotives.
QCAR	Network Rail New Measurement Train Class 43.
QETS	Network Rail Class 37.
RFSH	Wabtec Rail locomotives.
RTLO	Riviera Trains Class 47.
RVLO	Rail Vehicle Engineering locomotives.
WAAC	DB Schenker Class 67.
WABC	DB Schenker Class 67. RETB fitted.
WACC	DB Schenker Class 67 for hire to Chiltern Railways.

WAWC	DB Schenker Class 67 for hire to Arriva Trains Wales.
WBAT	DB Schenker Class 66.
WBBT	DB Schenker Class 66. RETB fitted.
WBLT	DB Schenker Industrial Class 66. Dedicated locomotives for Lickey Incline banking duties.
WBTT	DB Schenker Class 66. Fitted with tripcocks.
WCAT	DB Schenker Class 60.
WCBT	DB Schenker Class 60. Extended-range fuel tanks.
WDAM	DB Schenker Class 59.
WEAC	DB Schenker Class 90.
WEDC	DB Schenker Class 90 for hire to DRS.
WFAC	DB Schenker Class 92.
WFBC	DB Schenker Class 92 with commissioned TVM430 cab signalling equipment for use on High Speed 1.
WFCC	DB Schenker Class 92 for hire to DRS.
WGEE	DB Schenker Class 92 for export.
WQAA	DB Schenker stored locomotives Group 1A (short-term maintenance).
WQBA	DB Schenker stored locomotives Group 2 (unserviceable).
WQCA	DB Schenker stored locomotives Group 3 (unserviceable).
WQDA	DB Schenker stored locomotives Group 4 (awaiting disposal).
WSSC	DB Schenker Class 08/09.
XHAC	Direct Rail Services Classes 37/4, 47 & 57/3.
XNCE	Direct Rail Services Class 68 for hire to Chiltern Railways.
XHCK	Direct Rail Services Class 57/0.
XHHP	Direct Rail Services locomotives – holding pool.
XHIM	Direct Rail Services locomotives – Intermodal traffic.
XHNB	Direct Rail Services Class 47 for use on the Northern Belle.
XHNC	Direct Rail Services locomotives – nuclear traffic/general.
XHSS	Direct Rail Services stored locomotives.
XHVE	Direct Rail Services Class 68.
XHVT	Direct Rail Services Class 57/3 for hire to Virgin Trains.
XYPA	Mendip Rail Class 59/1.
XYPO	Mendip Rail Class 59/0.

7.4. ALLOCATION & LOCATION CODES

Allocation codes are used in this publication to denote the normal maintenance base ("depots") of each operational locomotive. However, maintenance may be carried out at other locations and also by mobile teams. The designation (S) denotes stored.

Code	Location	Depot Operator
BA	Basford Hall Yard (Crewe)	Freightliner
BH	Barrow Hill (Chesterfield)	Barrow Hill Engine Shed Society
BL*	Shackerstone, Battlefield Line	*Storage location only*
BM	Bournemouth	South West Trains
BN	Bounds Green (London)	East Coast
BO	Burton-upon-Trent	Nemesis Rail
BQ	Bury (Greater Manchester)	East Lancashire Rly Trust/Riley & Son (Railways)
CD	Crewe Down Holding Sidings	Riviera Trains

CE	Crewe International	DB Schenker Rail (UK)
CO	Coquelles (France)	Eurotunnel
CP	Crewe Carriage Shed	LNWR Company (part of Arriva)
CR	Crewe Gresty Bridge	Direct Rail Services
CS	Carnforth	West Coast Railway Company
EC	Edinburgh Craigentinny	East Coast
HT	Heaton (Newcastle)	Northern
KM	Carlisle Kingmoor	Direct Rail Services
KR	Kidderminster	Severn Valley Railway
LA	Laira (Plymouth)	First Great Western
LB	Loughborough Works	Wabtec Rail
LD	Leeds Midland Road	Freightliner Engineering
LE	Landore (Swansea)	First Great Western
LM	Long Marston (Warwickshire)	Motorail (UK)
LR	Leicester	UK Rail Leasing
LT	Longport (Stoke-on-Trent)	Electro Motive Diesel Services
MD	Merehead	Mendip Rail
NC	Norwich Crown Point	Abellio Greater Anglia
NL	Neville Hill (Leeds)	East Midlands Trains/Northern
NY	Grosmont (North Yorkshire)	North Yorkshire Moors Railway Enterprises
OO	Old Oak Common HST	First Great Western
PG	Peterborough	GB Railfreight
RU	Rugby	Colas Rail
SE	St Leonards (Hastings)	St Leonards Railway Engineering
SH	Southall (London)	West Coast Railway Co/Locomotive Services
SL	Stewarts Lane (London)	Southern/Belmond
SK	Swanwick Junction (Derbyshire)	Midland Railway Enterprises
TM	Tyseley Locomotive Works	Birmingham Railway Museum
TO	Toton (Nottinghamshire)	DB Schenker Rail (UK)
WH*	Washwood Heath (Birmingham)	Boden Rail Engineering/RMS Locotec
WN	Willesden (London)	London Overground
WO*	Wolsingham, Weardale Railway	RMS Locotec
YK	National Railway Museum (York)	National Museum of Science & Industry
ZA	RTC Business Park (Derby)	Railway Vehicle Engineering
ZB	Doncaster Works	Wabtec Rail
ZC	Crewe Works	Bombardier Transportation UK
ZD	Derby Works	Bombardier Transportation UK
ZG	Eastleigh Works	Arlington Fleet Services
ZH	Springburn Depot (Glasgow)	Knorr-Bremse Rail Systems (UK)
ZI	Ilford Works	Bombardier Transportation UK
ZJ	Stoke-on-Trent Works	Axiom Rail (Stoke)
ZK	Kilmarnock Works	Wabtec Rail Scotland
ZN	Wolverton Works	Knorr-Bremse Rail Systems (UK)
ZR	York (Holgate Works)	Network Rail

*= unofficial code.